PRAISE FOR
INTROVERT POWER

"This is such a good book! Laurie Helgoe has created an important guide to embracing one's inner life and claiming it as a rich source of power, creativity, and connectedness. Through concise yet pithy examples and exercises, she shows how to celebrate introversion and support yourself to thrive—shamelessly!"
—Camille Maurine, author of *Meditation Secrets for Women* and *Meditation 24/7*, creator of the "Moving Theater" process

"Laurie Helgoe's *Introvert Power* is a long overdue look at the power of introversion. We shouldn't think something is wrong with us if we shun the sometimes chaotic life of an extrovert. Many of the great intellectual, artistic, philosophical, and religious thinkers were introverts. Introversion can connect us to the source of our Being so we may remain grounded as we work in the world. If you have introvert inclinations and are doubting yourself, this is a must read. Or if you know someone who exhibits introvert symptoms, read this book before calling the shrink."
—Bhante Yogavacara Rahula, author of *One Night's Shelter: An Autobiography of an American Buddhist Monk*

INTROVERT
POWER

INTROVERT POWER

WHY YOUR
INNER LIFE IS YOUR
HIDDEN STRENGTH

Laurie Helgoe, PhD

SOURCEBOOKS, INC.®
NAPERVILLE, ILLINOIS

Published by Sourcebooks, Inc.
P.O. Box 4410, Naperville, Illinois 60567–4410
(630) 961–3900
Fax: (630) 961–2168
www.sourcebooks.com

Library of Congress Cataloging-in-Publication Data

Helgoe, Laurie A.
  Introvert power : why your inner life is your hidden strength / Laurie Helgoe.
    p. cm.
  ISBN 978-1-4022-1117-1 (trade pbk.)
  1. Introversion. I. Title.
  BF698.35.I59H45 2008
  155.2'32—dc22
                                    2008004967

Printed and bound in the United States of America.
BG 10 9 8 7 6 5 4 3 2 1

To Catherine, midwife to my introversion, ten years ago today.

To Barron, The One, twenty-five years into the best decision we've made.

Believe nothing.
No matter where you read it,
Or who said it,
Even if I have said it,
Unless it agrees with your own reason
And your own common sense.

—Buddha

INTROVERT POWER

Contents

Introduction

If you haven't been to a mosh pit, you've probably seen one in movies. A mob of people are crowded together, body to body, dancing and slamming into each other, usually at a live music club or concert. Occasionally, someone dives into the pit from the stage and "surfs" on the upraised arms of the crowd. The challenge of "moshing" is to work your way as close as possible to the band and to avoid getting trampled. Security guards keep watch in case such a thing happens, but any mosher will tell you that the pit is dangerous.

I've come to see the mosh pit as an apt description of American society—and of my childhood home. I was number nine out of ten bright, creative, and mostly LOUD kids. My dad, an eccentric genius, had wall-sized speakers in the living room that blared out classical music. When the family sang together, we sang five-part harmonies of the uncompromising Handel's *Messiah*. On Christmas Eve, we had a talent show and family service, and later tore into our presents all at once, paper and ribbons flying everywhere and voices crisscrossing the room shouting out "thank you!" and "just what I wanted!" These are happy memories, because there was a part for each of us. But instead of ripping paper and shouting, I sat in my corner with my pile of gifts and handled each as a treasure, slowly and carefully opening them, preserving the paper and lingering in the delight of discovery. I was meditating in the mosh pit.

However, when there were no gifts to open and everyone was competing for airtime, I felt invisible and became over-stimulated and anxious. My anxiety was not about the pressure to socialize; there were more than enough bodies to take care of that. I became anxious because I couldn't *think*, and, without my own mind, I felt like I was disintegrating. My solution was to retreat to my room and write. In my solitude I could regain contact with myself and become solid again.

I had a rich imagination; I wrote science fiction and developed secret codes with my little sister and a neighbor girl. Though the mosh pit was stressful, I knew that retreating was an option.

I lost this freedom when I entered school.

In first grade, I got scolded for hiding out in the bathroom with a couple of girls during recess. We were sprawled out on the floor, quietly engaged in the subversive practice of—yes, coloring. That's when I learned that my desire for quiet and solitude was bad.

I adapted. Years later, as a PhD candidate in clinical psychology, I didn't tell anyone that I was intimidated by the prospect of sitting in the room with a stranger. I wanted to be *under* the surface—not to have to get there through social exchange. Again, I adapted, found success as a psychologist, and had practiced for almost ten years when I first admitted to my analyst (and *myself*) how taxing the "social exchange," particularly with new clients, had been for me. This was the first time I had acknowledged the simple truth: I am an introvert.

My confession of introversion allowed me to rediscover the treasured self I had buried when I first stepped on the school bus. My analysis provided me the time and space I had craved, and I entered a personal renaissance. I took my first-ever personal retreat, letting my husband and little boys handle things while I indulged in the privacy of a remote B&B in the woods. I began a prolific period of writing, learned to craft candles, discovered poetry, and, for the first time, saw a world beyond the constrictions of my profession. Predictably, as I came alive, people around me—even my closest family members—got worried. What if I relinquished my hard-earned career to sell candles on the art fair circuit? What kind of crazy ideas was I getting from my analyst? It hurts when the self you most value becomes a source of worry. But once you tap into that self, the worry won't stop you.

What kept me going was the energy I discovered. For the first time since my carefree childhood days, I experienced *flow*. When I took my solitary walks, I felt I could walk forever, basking in the ample space for thought and imagination. I discovered the sky and drew on its vastness as a source of comfort.

The world opened to me during these walks, and I began to envision new possibilities for my life. The image of a piano keyboard came to my mind, and I recognized that I had only learned one note—I was an expert on that note, but there were so many more to discover. The sky reminded me that there was so much more than the limited corner of the world I had come to know. I was filled with desire, and that desire led me to new notes and new places.

I was transported by the power of introversion.

Since that opening, I have experienced the glamour of being a model, savored the power of holding an audience captive as a stage actor, wrote and directed mixed-media performances, accompanied my son on an Amazon expedition, and, most satisfying of all, realized my desire to become an author.

Here's a well-kept secret: Introversion is not defined by lack. Introversion, when embraced, is a wellspring of riches. It took me years to acknowledge this simple reality, to claim my home, and to value all it offers.

Perhaps you also feel most at home within. But you've probably also felt the pull to abandon this home—to set up house in the world of social interactions. Even if you only enjoy an occasional visit inside yourself, you may struggle to justify such an indulgence. Because extroversion lines up so well with American values, we introverts often deprive ourselves of what we most enjoy and thrive on. So, for all of you who draw energy from inside, behind, underneath, or away from it all, welcome home.

AMERICA THE EXTROVERTED

There's a lot to love about America—freedom, the melting pot of diversity, individualism—all attractive concepts, especially to an introvert. In fact, the introverts were probably the first to feel crowded in England and to daydream about all the space they would find in the New World. Peace! Quiet!

Fast-forward to the new millennium—and it has been a fast trip forward—in which we are more likely to associate America with office space than with "spacious skies." We have become an outward and upward society, conquering, building, competing, buying out, improving—extroverting. The squeaky wheels get greased, the ones who snooze lose, the best team wins, and the winner takes all.

In this culture of competition, it is no wonder that those of us who prefer introversion feel anxious. We are expected to "think on our feet," but we think best when we're still. We're pressured to join and keep up, when we'd rather follow an inner guide. And with the ever-multiplying multimedia—from pop-up ads on the Internet to phones that can reach us *everywhere*—the competition finds us where we live. Even the sacred introvert haven, the dark movie theatre, is now being invaded by *commercials!*

When introverts sense invasion, we instinctively shut down to protect our inner resources. But in doing so, we lose access to ourselves. From this defensive position, we may

DEFINING OUR TERMS

Introversion is an inward orientation to life, and *extroversion* (alternatively spelled *extraversion*) is an outward orientation. Though you probably use both introversion and extroversion, one of these orientations usually feels more like home—more comfortable, more interesting and more energizing—than the other. *Introverts* prefer introversion; we tend to gain energy by reflecting and expend energy when interacting. *Extroverts* have the opposite preference; they tend to gain energy by interacting and expend energy while reflecting.

feel that our only options are to practice extroversion, go underground, or go crazy.

Could it be that there's another alternative? Perhaps we could draw on our personal and communal strengths to *assert* introversion in our culture. Sound like a paradox? Yes—as paradoxical as meditating in a mosh pit.

INTROVERSION FOR ALL

According to the introverted psychiatrist Carl G. Jung, introversion and extroversion are two opposing forces within an individual. Jung was the first to identify these personality attitudes, one "characterized by orientation in life through subjective psychic contents" (introversion) and the other, "by concentration of interest on the external object" (extroversion). Isabel Briggs Myers and Katharine Cook Briggs, who developed the popular Myers-Briggs Type Indicator®, built on the idea that introverts prefer to focus on their own inner world, whereas extroverts prefer to focus on the outer world. But as the concepts of introversion and extroversion gained popularity, they began to lose their dynamic roots. We tend to see ourselves as introverted OR extroverted, rather than as a creative, evolving combination of the two.

It is this dynamism that makes introversion relevant to all of us. Whether the scale tips in the I direction and you call yourself an introvert, or you load up on the side of E, every one of us has some capacity for introversion. When a culture devalues these qualities, we are all reduced.

The way personal growth is supposed to progress, according to Jung, is that we first develop what comes naturally—introversion or extroversion. This specialization works well until later life, when the individual gets bored and wants to expand his or her range. But what happens when the introvert is discouraged or, worse, prohibited from practicing her specialty?

The introvert may adapt, but she walks around with a nagging sense of homelessness. She won't need to wait until midlife to become bored—she's bored already! It's hard enough to be in a career that doesn't fit, but for many introverts, the *life* doesn't fit.

For these introverts, what is needed is *not* a move toward extroversion, but as a friend of mine put it, an opportunity to "melt into introversion." This book is not about finding balance—we are really tired of doing that! Besides, finding balance assumes that we have been *allowed* to be fully introverted. We have not. This book is about embracing the power of introversion. It's about indulging, melting into, drinking in, immersing ourselves in the joy, the genius, and the power of who we naturally are—and not just on the occasional retreat, but in the living of our lives. Ironically, balance will only come to us if we forget about extroversion for awhile, and balance will only come to our society when we see and respect the introversion in all of us.

THE BIG LIE

Thanks to Jung and his successors, we have the tools to understand these qualities. We have a personality test to measure introversion and extroversion. The Myers-Briggs Type Indicator® (MBTI) has generated a vast amount of research on introversion and extroversion. Popular literature has emerged to explain how each of us can understand our personality preferences and use them to our advantage. But lies about introversion are so imbedded in the fabric of our culture that even the literature geared toward correcting misconceptions inadvertently promotes them.

The biggest lie is that introverts are in the minority, making up one-fourth or one-third of the population, depending on what you've read. Any introvert who has done a quick web search, attempting to find some company, has probably run across and even quoted these figures. But not only are these figures floating around the Web, they are also repeatedly quoted in the self-help books many of us use as resources.

When I started my research for this book, I wanted to know where these statistics came from. I wanted to find the research that the books were quoting. So I went to the source: the *MBTI® Manual (©2003),* a regularly-updated compendium for the research on introversion, extroversion, and the other personality dimensions measured by the MBTI®. But what I found was quite different.

The first large-scale population study of the MBTI® revealed that introverts make up a good *half* (50.7 percent) of the population (and if you want to split hairs, we seem to be in the *majority*). This study, the largest to date, was conducted in 1998. A more recent population study, reported in the *MBTI® Step II Manual,* puts introverts a little further into the majority: 57 percent, compared to 43 percent extroverts.

It took me much longer to find the source of the claim that introverts make up only a third of the population. Isabel Myers made this estimate when the MBTI® was being developed— prior to *1962!*

How can we be so far off?

As much as research shows the contrary, the belief that introverts are in the minority has stuck. After all, in America, extroversion is *what we value.* And we see what we value. So we see extroverts everywhere, and we no longer notice the introverts everywhere. Sometimes we even miss the one looking back at us in the mirror. We might tell ourselves that *introverts are naturally less visible than extroverts.* This lie is as insidious and damaging as the lie about our numbers. Perhaps a better way to put it is that we are less *seen* in America. Go to Japan, for example, and, despite the massive population, an introverted businessperson is more likely to be noticed than a "fast talker."

In America, we think of introverts as withdrawn loners, quiet and scared. We readily diagnose a preference for looking inward as stemming from depression, anxiety, or antisocial tendencies. We don't know what introversion really is, and we interact with introverts all day without realizing it.

We've got it all wrong.

REVIVING YOUR INTROVERSION

From a young age, most of us are taught the value of social skills. We learn how to introduce ourselves, how to smile and be polite. We are told to be friendly and make friends. These are all useful abilities to develop. But how many of us are taught the value of solitude skills? How many of us are taught to protect our boundaries, to foster imagination, to be alone? How many of us are encouraged to withdraw from social activity and nurture the life of the mind?

This book is here to provide that missing training and support. We'll examine how introversion may have gotten away from you, and how to get it back. We'll deconstruct the extroversion assumption, and see how it manifests in everyday conversations, judgments, and ideas about work and play. As you are freed to reclaim your preference, you will be amazed at the power you feel. Life will flow in a way you hadn't thought was possible. You may find yourself asking: "Is this okay?" "Can things be this easy?"

As this transformation occurs at the individual level—this simple reclaiming of your home—you'll notice your world changing. I think you're going to like it.

Welcome.

WHAT'S INSIDE

Introvert Power provides an alternative to the extroversion training you've been receiving all your life. As unnatural as extroversion has felt to introverts, we've gotten used to it. Rather than putting a thin coat of introversion over layers of extroverted thinking, *Introvert Power* asks you to strip down your thinking first and then dip into your true colors. The book is divided into five parts, each essential to our retraining and best experienced in sequence.

In Part One, *Antisocial, Weird, or Displaced?* we take on—and take apart—the beliefs we've adopted about introversion, along with our culturally determined assumptions about what is healthy. We look at mistaken associations between introversion and mental illness, and confront our society's taboo against solitude. You'll meet two introvert styles, represented by Shadow Dwellers and Accessible Introverts, and learn how these styles have developed in the context of an alienating society. Then we start looking at what's real: our numbers, our influence on current trends, and the economic power we exert. Finally, we look at societies that favor introversion and what we can learn from them.

Part Two, *The Introvert's Wish List,* is the melting into introversion section. In these chapters, we indulge in our wishes for private space, time to think, routine retreats, passionate observation, and real intimacy. Though the process may feel like a guilty indulgence, we'll see why such pleasures are in fact essential to introverts and healing to society as a whole.

In Part Three, *Standing Still in a Loud World,* we move into the areas that have become defined by extroversion and look at how to bring an introvert tempo into the mix. You'll learn how to create space in conversations and how to just say no to parties—or how to hang out, introvert-style. We deal with work and the people who interrupt us. We sort out how to be there for the people we love while remaining loyal to ourselves. And we confront the downside of introversion, and how to know when we need a window out.

The final section, *Outing the Introvert,* takes us one step further, from introvert restoration to introvert renaissance. We take ownership of our society, educating rather than apologizing, acting with introvert integrity rather than conformity or indifference, and expressing, in our own way, the richness within us. We consider when extroversion is natural for us and, fully rooted in introversion, we relinquish the defensive stance that once restricted our freedom. We begin to meditate in the mosh pit and, as we do, the pit transforms into a house of meditation; the extroverted slamming no longer pushes us off balance, and the rhythms of introversion and extroversion complement each other in a new dance.

INTROVERT VOICES

My voice will always be limited in capturing your private experience, so I supplement my words here with the voices of a diverse group of introverts. I polled the introverts in my world, as well as subscribers to my website, www.wakingdesire.com (see also, www.introvertpower.com). A group of voices emerged: a college student from Puerto Rico who makes films in her spare time; a minister with a generative mind and minimalist lifestyle; a high school sophomore who obtains permission to doodle in her classes; a professional comedian; a sampling of accountants, artists, government employees, musicians, conservationists, health professionals, and writers. These contributors welcomed the opportunity to *write* their thoughts—extroverted techniques were not used in the making of this book—and struck me with their honesty and insight. Many appreciated being asked. The voices of introverted heroes—literary, historical, popular, and lesser known—also enrich the pages ahead.

Regardless of how many introvert perspectives I can provide, however, it is your voice that I hope to inspire.

Part I:
Antisocial, Weird, or Displaced?

Chapter 1: The Mistaken Identity

To be yourself in a world that is constantly trying to make you something else is the greatest accomplishment.

—Ralph Waldo Emerson

"He's thin and white…if he's tall he's got bad posture."

"Not particularly attractive, ungainly, with skin problems—would be first underweight and then (later in life) overweight."

"Nerdy."

"Geeky."

"Conservative style, neutral colors."

These are some descriptions of what an introvert looks like. What is alarming is that these descriptions all come from introverts! When the same people describe themselves, the picture changes:

"My physical appearance is…exotic. Light green-blue slanted eyes and high cheekbones."

"Natural blonde."

"I'm overweight, tanned skin, big, round, and dark brown eyes."

"Somewhat tall, reasonably attractive considering age."

"Brown curly hair—I look like I'm from another country."

What stood out to me as I polled these people was the sterile and colorless quality of the archetypal introvert, contrasted by the colorized descriptions of the self-identified introverts. The stereotyped introvert is often seen as introvert by default when, in fact, introversion is defined as a *preference*. Introverts generally prefer a rich inner life to an expansive social life; we would rather talk intimately with a close friend than share stories with a group; and we prefer to develop our ideas internally rather than interactively.

So how have we jumped from these preferences to images of a cowering, reclusive weirdo? Iris Chang commented, "Whatever is not commonly seen is condemned as alien." We have lost our eyes for introversion. As we discussed in the introduction, introverts make up *more than half* of the population, yet we assume that introverts are an occasional deviation—the geeks in the shadows.

Introversion, by definition, is not readily seen. Introverts keep their best stuff inside—that is, until it is ready. And this drives extroverts crazy! The explanation for the introvert's behavior—*and there must be an explanation for this behavior, say the extroverts*—is that he or she is antisocial, out of touch, or simply a snob.

Because introverts are trickier to read, it is easy to project our fears and negative biases onto this preference. And it's not just extroverts who do this. As my informal poll revealed, we often make similar assumptions about other introverts, and—most troubling of all—about ourselves! One of the introverts I polled is a striking beauty. She described her physical appearance as "OK." Another very attractive introvert described herself as "the status quo." These downplayed descriptions may reflect a tendency to focus less on externals, but we also tend to downplay our very personalities—the style we *prefer*. For example, do you ever jokingly or apologetically admit to being antisocial, or view yourself as boring in relation to your chatty associates? Do you beat yourself up for not joining in? Do you worry that something is wrong with you; that you're missing out; that who you are naturally is a problem needing correction?

Your nature is not the problem. The problem is that you have become *alienated* from your nature—from your power source. As Isabel Briggs Myers discussed in her book, *Gifts Differing,* "The best-adjusted people are the 'psychologically patriotic,' who are glad to be what they are." For introverts this means, "Their loyalty goes to their own inner principle and derives from it a secure and unshakable orientation to life."

> *I wondered if I was perhaps anti-social, or maybe even flawed.*
>
> —Suzanne, Oregon

But we *have* been shaken. To reclaim the power of introversion, we must first deconstruct the assumptions we make about who we are.

THE OPPOSITE OF SOCIAL IS NOT ANTISOCIAL

Of all the assumptions made about introverts, the idea that we are *antisocial* is the most ridiculous. The term "antisocial" actually refers to sociopathy (or antisocial personality disorder), a condition in which a person lacks a social conscience. This has nothing to do with introversion. Introverts are often deeply concerned about the human condition; they just tend to look within for answers. Ironically, the classic sociopath is quite charming and socially engaging, but lacks the *inner* capacity to feel empathy and guilt.

This is a great example of how our vision tricks us. An introvert deep in thought will *look* self-absorbed, whether he's thinking about world hunger or working out how to hack into someone's bank account. An engaging extrovert will *look* friendly, whether he really cares about your day or is trying to pick your pocket. Therapists are reluctant to apply the diagnosis of antisocial personality disorder until there is clear evidence for it, because it is a serious problem with a poor prognosis. Enjoying your own company does not warrant any diagnosis, but this one is especially cruel.

But are we just talking semantics here? When we use "anti-social" in this way, we really mean not social, or *asocial*—the correct term for someone who does not like to interact with people. So would it be fair to say that introverts are asocial?

Wrong again.

THE OPPOSITE OF SOCIAL IS NOT INTROVERTED

An introvert may *feel* asocial when pressured to go to a party that doesn't interest her. But for her, the event does not promise meaningful interaction. In fact, she knows that the party will leave her feeling *more* alone and alienated. Her social preference may be to stay home and reflect on a conversation with a friend, call that friend, and come to an understanding that is meaningful to her. Or she might indulge in the words of a favorite author, feeling a deep connection with a person she has never met. From the perspective of a partygoer, this introvert may appear to be asocial, when, in fact, the introvert is interacting in a much different way.

Because the introvert is oriented to the inner world, she "takes to heart" something a good friend says and needs time to reflect before responding. This can happen during a relaxed talk, but, for the introvert, the understanding deepens during the time *between* conversations. If we think of each person as having a finite amount of interpersonal space, an extrovert is more like a hotel—able to

> **Q:** What would you like extroverts to understand about you?
> **A:** That we are social, too. It [socializing] just takes energy away from us and we need to recharge after a certain amount of time. Our need to retreat is not a statement about them or our relationship with them.
> —Lisa, North Carolina

accommodate a large number of interactions that come and go. Note that I said *interactions,* not people. Extroverts are often able to accommodate more people as well, but because extroverts wrap up interactions *in the* interaction, even a close friend may check in and check out as needed. An introvert may have the same square footage, but each meaningful interaction is reserved in its own luxury suite, awaiting the follow-up interaction. Bookings are more limited.

A related assumption about introverts is that we are socially incompetent. Are you starting to see a pattern? Assumptions about introversion usually link the preference with some kind of *lack* or disorder. So let's get this one over with too. Just as extroverts can have poor social skills (think of the raucous, obnoxious socializer), introverts can be socially savvy. Introverts often choose "people professions" as their life work. I have been wrong too many times to assume that an outgoing social leader is an extrovert. The introverted leader may check out for refueling and relish alone time after work, but be quite "out there" in her public role. Stories abound of high-profile introverts who chill out to read a book, watch golf on TV, or take a walk.

So, being an introvert does not mean you're antisocial, asocial, or socially inept. It does mean that you are oriented to ideas—whether those ideas involve you with people or not. It means that you prefer spacious interactions with fewer people. And it means that, when you converse, you are more interested in sharing ideas than in talking about people and what they're doing. In a conversation with someone sharing gossip, the introvert's eyes glaze over and his brow furrows as he tries to comprehend how this conversation could interest anyone. This is not because the introvert is morally superior—he just doesn't *get it.* As we've discussed, introverts are energized and excited by ideas. Simply talking about people, what they do and who they know, is noise for the introvert. He'll be looking between the lines for some meaning, and this can be hard work! Before long, he'll be looking for a way out of the conversation.

But when an introvert is hanging out with a friend, sharing ideas, he is in his element. The conversation is "mind to mind" rather than "mouth to mouth." Extroverts share ideas too, but the ideas are secondary to the interaction, and develop *between* the two people as they talk. The focal point is external. For introverts, the focal point is internal, with each participant bringing the other inside and working things out there. A good conversation leaves an introvert feeling more connected, but also personally richer.

Understanding the *location* of interactions puts introverts back on the map. Extroverts understandably need more face-to-face time, because that's where the interaction is located. Introverts need more *between* time—between words in a conversation and between conversations—because the interaction is located within.

WE ARE NOT SNOBS

While this is an assumption some introverts like—being a snob is better than being *impaired*—it ultimately hurts us. Think of a group of Extrovert Moms gathered together at a Little League game, excitedly chatting and enjoying the action. In comes Introvert Mom who, after a full day of work, wants nothing more than to savor the game—all by herself. She sits off a bit from everyone else, stretching her feet onto the bleacher bench, and may even have a book to indulge in as the team warms up. She might enjoy watching the people around her, but she has no energy to interact.

What are the Extrovert Moms thinking? Because they are oriented to people, they will likely assume that Introvert Mom is, too—which means they see Introvert Mom as not liking people (what we know now as asocial) or being a "snob," thinking she's too good for the Extrovert Moms. More likely, Introvert Mom *is not thinking about them at all!* She is just doing something she likes to do.

The snob assumption is an extrovert personalization of the introvert's behavior: she's not just doing something for herself;

she's dissing *us*. This misunderstanding may lead to gossip and suspicious looks. If Introvert Mom feels this hostile energy, she may become defensive and further withdraw to protect herself, only confirming to the Extrovert Moms that she is indeed a snob.

An introvert who regards herself as a snob, and looks down on extroverts as superficial or shallow *loses,* rather than gains, strength. This is because her focus moves outward, away from her power source. Though she may think she is being unkind to the extroverts around her, she is actually being very unkind to herself. The snob myth perpetuates the idea that her introversion is a snub of those around her, rather than something she enjoys and values.

WE ARE DIFFERENT—DIFFERENT FROM EXTROVERTS

Introverts are drawn to worlds more exotic or complex than what is immediately available. Whether we like hanging out in fantasy, spiritual contemplation, mental investigation, artistic creation, or wilderness exploration, we may seem different, out of touch, or just weird. Out of touch? *Yes—* really not wanting to be touched or otherwise intruded on at the moment. Weird? Only to people who want to touch or otherwise intrude on us.

We are different from the other 43 percent of the population, but that's as much as we can say about introverts being abnormal. Yet, there is a long and stubborn association between introversion and mental illness. Though the MBTI® describes preferences in healthy terms, some personality tests use the term "introversion" to describe problematic symptoms. The idea of extroversion as normal—and introversion as abnormal—is so prevalent in our culture that it has seeped into our mental health system.

There are a number of reasons for this association that have little to do with the actual mental health of the individual.

First, introverts are higher users of mental health services. Why? They like looking inside! For many introverts, therapy is attractive and exciting. They are not afraid of what they'll find—they're already familiar with the territory.

Secondly, extroverts often incorrectly assume that introverts are suffering. Introverts *internalize* problems; we like to take things inside and work on them there. Extroverts prefer to *externalize* and deal with problems interactively. Because of this difference, introverts may seem psychologically burdened, while extroverts spread the burden around and seem healthier—from an *extroverted* standpoint. But note that I said introverts *like* to take problems inside. Sure, an introvert can overdo it, but so can the extrovert who feels compelled to express every unresolved thought or emotion. The former gets depressed or anxious and goes to therapy; the latter sends *others* to therapy.

> *But now it seems that adults like me, particularly single women who much prefer familiar surroundings and one-on-one communications with people, are encouraged to work on our "issues," our social anxiety, and to get "out there" and learn the artful skill of making idle conversation with strangers. But why? In order to mingle well at parties.*
>
> *—Suzanne, day job: outreach worker for a public defender team; passions: all things introverted, but "first and foremost" reading*

Finally, introverts can become the carriers of family and societal problems. Family systems theory talks about the *identified patient* as the family member who carries the pathology that the rest of the family denies. The alcoholic parent and the volatile marriage are not addressed, but the introverted child who takes it all inside becomes "ill" and goes to therapy. Taking on the pathology of others is a huge risk for introverts and one we will address in later chapters. As a therapist myself, I find that it is often the healthiest family member who enters therapy, because he is willing to look at the limitations of his own reality and risk change.

THE ABANDONMENT OF THE INTERNAL

Though introverts may be more curious about psychology, psychology has become less curious about our inner lives. In the early 1900s, American practitioners were looking for more objective measures of mental health, and the new trend of radical behaviorism met the need. Suddenly, instead of focusing on what was hidden—the purview of psychoanalysis—behaviorism dismissed anything that could not be observed. All we needed to know was what goes in (stimulus) and what happens (response). So, the therapist's focus shifted from the client's disclosures of feeling to an external measure, such as the number of times she smiles during the session. (This is an actual example from my graduate training!)

Consider how this plays out for the introverted client. She acknowledges feeling burdened and seeks help. She is readily diagnosed for her internal focus, but then the tables turn: she is deprived of the opportunity to seek inner solutions. Her "cure" involves shifting her focus to external realities—using her least developed capacity.

Though radical behaviorism has gradually given way to cognitive-behaviorism, which does acknowledge inner processes, the value of external over internal has remained. And insurance companies loved the idea. Physicians, as well as therapists, are no longer paid to be curious about what's inside and to search for a cause—we are rewarded for finding the shortest path between symptoms and solution, and if we don't get it right, the attitude is "they can always come back and you can try something else."

So, if we've decided that what's inside is out of the picture, introverts will look inferior. The introvert's strong suit is inside. There, he is comfortable, confident, and content. By contrast, the extrovert "inside" might not look so good—he becomes anxious and awkward when he's not out doing something or talking to someone. But who cares? Just as we don't see the strength of the introvert, we don't notice the weakness of the extrovert. What's inside is locked away in the black box.

From the outside, the introvert may not look so good, and we *do* care about this. If a child stays quiet in the context of extroverted friends, or even prefers time alone, a parent may worry and even send her to therapy. She might be thrilled— she'll finally get to talk about the stuff she cares about, and without interruption! But if the therapist concludes that the child has a social phobia, the treatment of choice is to increasingly *expose* her to the situations she fears. This behavioral treatment is effective for treating phobias — if that is truly the problem. If it's not the problem, and the child just likes hanging out inside better than chatting, she'll have a problem soon. Her "illness" now will be an internalized self-reproach: "Why don't I enjoy this like everyone else?" The otherwise carefree child learns that something is wrong with her. She not only is pulled away from her home, she is supposed to *like it*. Now she is anxious and unhappy, confirming the suspicion that she has a problem.

Under normal conditions, the introvert places less value on what is outside, and puts less energy there. Briggs Myers described this outside self as the Aide to a General:

> The introvert's General is inside the tent, working on matters of top priority. The Aide is outside fending off interruptions...If people do not realize that there is a General in the tent who far outranks the Aide they have met, they may easily assume that the Aide is in sole charge. This is a regrettable mistake. It leads not only to an underestimation of the introvert's abilities but also to an incomplete understanding of his wishes, plans, and point of view. The only source for such information is the General.

Though the metaphor of a General may or may not fit your tastes, it is an image of power. Whether your tent is a busy laboratory or a vast library, a creative studio or spiritual sanctuary, your inner world is the place where the action is, where your heart starts pumping, and your potential expands. And like the General in the tent, we can move the world. But first, we need to recognize that someone is there.

WE ARE INTROVERTS

What constitutes an introvert is quite simple. We are a vastly diverse group of people who prefer to look at life from the inside out. We gain energy and power through inner reflection, and get more excited by ideas than by external activities. When we converse, we listen well and expect others to do the same. We think first and talk later. Writing appeals to us because we can express ourselves without intrusion, and we often prefer communicating this way. Even our brains look different than those of extroverts.

In 1967, psychologist Hans Eysenck published his "arousal theory" of introversion and extroversion, which predicted that introverts would have higher levels of cortical arousal than extroverts. In other words, introvert brains would be more stimulated on an ongoing basis; extrovert brains would be quieter. This would explain why introverts pull away from environmental stimuli while extroverts seek out more.

To test the theory, researchers have looked at various measures of mental stimulation, such as blood flow and electrical activity, in the brains of introverts and extroverts. The consistent finding was that, as predicted, introvert brains were busier than extrovert brains. After summarizing this research, the writers of the 2003 *MBTI*® *Manual* concluded: "Introverts appear to do their best thinking in anticipation rather than on the spot; it *now seems clear* [emphasis mine] that this is because their minds are so naturally abuzz with activity that they need to shut out external distractions in order to prepare their ideas." So it is impossible to fully and fairly understand introversion without looking inside. We aren't just going *away*, we're going *toward* something. Extroverts may have more going on socially, but we've got more going on upstairs.

The simple preference for inner life, when honored, opens the introvert to a richness and complexity that is highly personal and is indeed *personality* with the exclamation point! Instead of defining—or diagnosing—introversion from the outside, let's look at a description by a man who mined the depths of inner life, Carl Jung:

> For him self-communings are a pleasure. His own world is a safe harbour, a carefully tended and walled-in garden, closed to the public and hidden from prying eyes. His own company is the best. He feels at home in his world, where the only changes are made by himself. His best work is done with his own resources, on his own initiative, and in his own way…His retreat into himself is not a final renunciation of the world, but a search for quietude, where alone it is possible for him to make his contribution to the life of the community.

As much as introverts may be misunderstood or devalued, people are drawn to the richness we conceal and enjoy the products we create in our "tents." The reclusive songwriter entertains through the computer audio system developed by introverts. Voices of introverts speak through books so varied we can be entertained by just looking at the titles in a bookstore. Introverts make us think and ask questions. We fall silent as the quiet person in the room reveals wisdom from his inner reservoir.

Introverts, it is time for us to claim our space, our time, and our vitality. If the rest of you want what we've got, welcome! But don't come over—*get an inner life!* We Are Introverts, and we are going home.

Chapter 2:
Alone Is Not a
Four-Letter Word

─────────────────────────

The great omission in American life is solitude; not loneliness, for this is an alienation that thrives most in the midst of crowds, but that zone of time and space, free from the outside pressures, which is the incubator of the spirit.

—Marya Mannes

You're headed home on a Friday evening. Exhausted from a week of interacting, performing, and responding to others, you relish the prospect of time alone, cuddling up or stretching, reading or puttering—inhabiting the silent space. You stop at the bookstore and run into an acquaintance who asks what you are doing tonight. You tell her, and she looks worried. You take in the look of worry and start to wonder if there is something wrong with you. Everyone else seems to want to go out.

Let's say your self-doubt prompts you to go out, and you stop by a party that a friend is hosting. Your friends are surprised and happy to see you, validating your choice. But soon into the greetings, you feel as if you've left something behind. You start regretting the choice "everyone else" encouraged. Feeling the "alienation that thrives most in the midst of crowds," you long to be alone, free to think your own thoughts and move to your own rhythm. But you haven't been here long enough to leave; you feel trapped.

This "alienation of association" is widespread in our culture, but it has no diagnostic label. Regardless of how dead we feel in a crowd, we cling to the uniquely American assumption that associating is good and necessary and solitude is suspect. Let's imagine the above scenario going the opposite way:

When you stop by the bookstore, you tell the acquaintance you are going to a party. She looks worried, and expresses concern about all you'll miss. She comments, "You've been waiting all week for some time to yourself; why would you compromise that?" If you've been spending a lot of time with people, she might express concern that you are avoiding time alone and suggest that you might be depressed.

While such a response is unlikely, it's a comment an introvert would appreciate. For an introvert, interacting in a group setting *does* mean missing out. Where there is too much input, the introvert misses his mind, his subjectivity, his freedom, his very potential. The high-stimulus social environment, the "where it's at on a Friday night," this apparent "more," becomes a prison to the introvert. He can't wait to be free—to get out and away from the noise, the talk, the interference with his inner process. Yet, the discrepancy between his mood and his surroundings may lead to self-criticism, the hallmark of depression.

> Solitude is not rejection, isolation, depression, or a sign of spiritual desolation.
>
> —Don, Unitarian Universalist minister and avid baseball fan

It would be wise to be concerned about the introvert who is deprived of solitude. Is she neglecting herself due to depression? Is she falling victim to guilt and self-reproach? Does she feel cut off from pleasure? Does she feel dead?

"Where it's at" for the introvert is in the expansive space of solitude. This is where the introvert is fed, calmed, moved, and inspired. Our training tells us to worry about solitude and to limit it, and our language places the social world at the center: we withdraw (*from* something) or retreat (*from* something) or isolate ourselves (*from* something). We have a verb for interacting with people—socializing—but have no single, affirmative verb to describe being alone. We tend to view alone time either as a problem to be overcome or a luxury we cannot afford—not as a staple we all need. We're not just social animals. We are solitary animals as well.

But if we look closer, we discover that *many* verbs capture solitary experience: daydreaming, meditating, fantasizing, calculating, planning, thinking, theorizing, imagining, praying, observing, composing, reflecting, inventing—and this list doesn't even include typically solitary activities like reading, drawing, researching, and writing. Solitude is not *lack*. As understood by Taoist practitioners, solitude is a "fertile void," an open door to a world overflowing with possibilities.

In another sense, most of what we do is solitary. We may have lots of people around, but the path each of us takes is our own. Yet, the expectation that we attach ourselves to others leaves many of us feeling lonely and alienated. What if we referred to social interaction as withdrawal from solitude? What if we viewed solitude as the center of experience and made sure that our kids were equipped to handle it?

Solitude is indeed "the great omission in American life." We are told to have family values, to be a team player, to have a huge wireless network. More is better and there is never enough. How did we get so far away from ourselves?

THE CULTURE OF MORE

American consumerism relies on this assumption: If only you had _____, you would have the life you desire. That shiny new car will make you better looking, happier, and more successful. More products will provide you more time, which you can fill by purchasing

> *In any ultimate sense, we are alone, and the sooner we accept it the sooner we can move on to life's real work: making a difference and becoming a blessing to the large number of people we know who are hurting and are less fortunate.*
>
> —Phil, Minnesota

more products. And, to clinch the sale, the commercial reminds us that everybody else already has one.

We have become a culture of "everybody else." Through our constantly expanding media channels, we can know what people are (supposedly) buying, how people are (supposedly) behaving, and what expectations others (supposedly) have for us. Reality television further erodes our sense of privacy and personal space: not only are the participants in our living room, but we're also in theirs!

In the typical American sitcom, people walk into each other's homes or apartments without knocking, flop on the couch, and start talking about their problems. Hip adults mingle in an ensemble of friends—a group of people who are interchangeably important to each other. Intrusion is the norm; if one friend leaves the room, another one enters; cool people are never alone. No matter if the friend is annoying or selfish; more is better.

Having more friends is equated with more fun, even more value. In a democratic society, more popular means more power. The buzzword of the '80s, "networking," became the ticket to success. In an increasingly public society, the emphasis shifts from quality to visibility; from good products to good marketing; from knowing to being known. There is no time; we need to "git 'r done" and "get out there." Is it any wonder that anxiety disorders have become the common cold of American life? We live much of our lives in panic mode, grasping for more without considering why. We're like children running into the streets to grab the candy thrown from the parade float, only to realize that the cheap morsels taste funny.

This "more" mode convinces us that solitude and reflection are too costly to risk. The parade is moving on and we *need that candy!* And if you're trying to be a success, you need to throw out as much as possible—flood the Internet with your message, pop up on everyone's screen, reach the people.

In a great little book titled *Purple Cow,* marketing analyst Seth Godin argues that more advertising is no longer better, that people no longer see or hear the flood of messages coming their way. Instead of mass marketing a product, he advocates creating a remarkable product—a purple cow—that sells because it's *not* a part of the more. His wisdom rings true for anyone who is sick of seeing penis enlargement spam on his computer screen.

Though a different kind of "more" comes with solitude, we benefit from the "less" side of solitude as well. For an introvert especially, movement away from the group allows access to a more independent, questioning, and honest voice—a voice that could make all the difference.

THE THREAT OF SOLITUDE

In a competitive culture, it helps to know what others are up to. Once you find out what others are doing, you can figure out how to do better—just better enough to get the business. But what happens when the competition doesn't let you in? You might get nervous, thinking that the other party is withholding something really big or planning some kind of takeover. The solitary party is going to get ahead, or worse. The reflexive attitude becomes, "something is being planned, and it might hurt me."

Although most introverts seek time alone as an *alternative* to people and competition, solitude is a power source for the introvert. And for someone wanting to exert control, solitude is indeed threatening. Many sales schemes rely on "today only" impulse purchases because "sleeping on it" will help you realize that you don't need the product. Cults gain their power by depriving members of any time alone. Clients in my office comment on what a difference it makes to have time to think, and value psychotherapy for its attention to inner processes. As inner strength builds, people find the courage to leave abusive relationships, to embark on new challenges, and to ask for what they want.

Every now and then, a disturbed loner misuses the power of solitude, feeding paranoia and planning destruction. These are the private figures that get public attention, and they do harm to introverts everywhere, contributing to our collective fear of solitude. But, by definition, introverts are not preoccupied with people and external events. They are drawn to ideas and concepts, and are able to explore these freely in solitude. More often, a tendency to pull inward is associated with a *lower* risk of violence. On the Minnesota Multiphasic Personality Inventory, for example, the *social introversion* scale is considered an *inhibitory scale*—one of the indicators that, when elevated, is associated with lower levels of delinquency.

The potentially violent loner is, ironically, externally focused. Rather than accepting and enjoying his preference for solitude, he focuses on his resentment of the group, seeing himself as a solo victim entitled to revenge. When this happens, solitude can become dangerous indeed, leaving room for his paranoid distortions and growing hatred. Here's the rub: the very distortions that place him outside of the group are ones we perpetuate in our society. The introvert is not a minority; at least *half* of us are on a similar plane. Half of us get worn out when we are around people for too long. Half of us are bored—some, to tears—by gossip. Half of us get an energy boost from reflective time. Beyond that, Jung would argue that half of every *individual* is introverted. Any extrovert who takes the MBTI® will notice that, though her score for extroversion is higher than the one for introversion, she's got some introversion. And, according to Jung, what isn't being used in conscious life is resting in the unconscious, ready to emerge as the individual grows.

The same is true for introverts, of course: there's a latent extrovert in there. The difference is, those of us on the introvert side are more often encouraged to jump right over our first choice and rouse up the extrovert.

INTROVERSION INTERRUPTED

Perhaps there is no better way to feel the pulse of society's values than to look at how we raise our children. As a psychologist, I have yet to see a child brought in for therapy because he is too social and his parents are concerned that he seems to have little access to his inner life. Yet, child after child is brought in for not talking enough, only having a few friends, and enjoying time alone—for being *introverted*. To be fair, many of these kids have problems. But often, the problem is not the kid.

Children today are largely raised in group settings, from daycare to preschool to school, and in their free time, we schedule play dates or push them to hang out with the neighborhood friends. In service of the "more is better" rule, parents strive to get more involved and see that the children are doing more. This ethic produces children who are monitored, structured, scheduled—and stressed. When a child says, "I'm bored!" we take this as a demand to entertain. Yet boredom is a necessary precursor to creativity. Children who cannot tolerate boredom and solitude become stimulus addicts, choosing the quick filler over the richness of possibility. When a child does seek refuge from overstimulation, retreating into solitude, parents are more likely to regard this as a problem than as a healthy way of recharging.

> *I grew up in a family of introverts. We read at the dinner table. My husband thinks we're wacked.*
>
> —Margit, North Carolina

And when a child enters school, there is no place to hide. Schools have responded to intellectually gifted children who are understimulated in the classroom, but we have yet to respond to the overstimulated introvert. I see some of these children in therapy. They are not hyperactive or unfocused. They just find the classroom too noisy and are annoyed by the kids who *are* hyperactive or disruptive. These clients predictably propose a very simple solution: "If only I could study by myself, I'd be fine." One of the teens I worked with told me about how she loves to take tests, because it is quiet and everyone is occupying their own space. School administrators have allowed her to pass, despite failing grades, because of her record-high test scores. Yet they have made no accommodation to provide the quiet she craves. Some of these overstimulated children opt for the "dumb class" because at least there are fewer kids, some thrive in homeschool programs, and others find help through psychiatric channels. Most learn to do without solitude and adapt to the noisy environment, carrying that nagging feeling of homelessness that haunts many introverts.

Each one of these solutions comes at a cost. Is it better to part with your introversion or to accept a diagnosis that allows you to have it as long as you see it as a problem? The introverted child's plea for solitude seems to be either unheeded or *treated*.

> [In solitude] I'm alone with my head. I feel liberated and I don't need to pretend anything for anyone.
>
> —Cecilia, Puerto Rico

Then what happens when the child comes home needing to decompress? Many kids today run to a computer or video screen. I ran across an article from a 1996 newsletter from the American Academy of Pediatrics with the title, "Are we facing a generation of 'Internet introverts'?" The implication was that the Internet was creating introverts, an apparently dangerous outcome. Parents hearing such warnings responsibly pull their kids off the computer and tell them to call a friend. Sure, video games and the Internet can become a rut, but perhaps it's the only place where many introverted children can preserve some privacy and independence in their overscheduled lives. If the child is seeking solitude, perhaps a better response is to limit computer time and *leave the child alone.*

Even introverts who find support often feel deprived. One such introvert is the daughter of a friend of mine. She's bright and creative, does well in school, and her parents allow her the freedom to pursue her solitary passions. This girl had the opportunity to take the MBTI®, and when she read the results, describing her introvert preferences in healthy terms, she shed tears of relief. The power of seeing herself in this mirror, reflecting back the best part of her, was overwhelming. She saw herself, and she loved what she saw.

THE FEAR OF SOLITUDE

Though social pressures discourage being alone, we introverts also erect roadblocks of our own. We get busy, and the more distant solitude becomes, the more we avoid it. As we avoid solitude, the introverted part of ourselves becomes unhappy. We sense this inner grief, and we don't want to deal with it.

The reality, even for introverts, is that solitude is often unpleasant at first. The unpleasant sensation may be the surfacing of feelings we've been ignoring, or fear of "coming down" from the stimulation of our people-filled lives. This fear is common even when our people-filled lives are *overstimulating*. Being overstimulated may feel bad, but it's a bad that we're used to.

I had the privilege of attending a workshop on *Time Shifting* by Stephen Rechtschaffen, founder of the Omega Institute and frequent retreat facilitator. He observed that it is common for people to become depressed at first when they begin a retreat. Rather than catching the first plane home, he encourages individuals to allow the feeling, to let it rise and fall like a wave. Once they settle into solitude, they remember why they came and they find what they came for—and more.

I often have this experience with my writing. I sit down, expecting it to feel good right away. Instead I feel empty, bored, and wonder what ever made me think I could write. As writers learn, we do best when we stay with it, and sometimes staying with it hurts. But as I sink into the space of thought and imagination, the void becomes fertile, and the longer I stay, the more I want to stay.

> I have never felt lonesome, or in the least oppressed by a sense of solitude, but once, and that was a few weeks after I came to the woods, when, for an hour, I doubted if the near neighborhood of man was not essential to a serene and healthy life. To be alone was something unpleasant. But I was at the same time conscious of a slight insanity in my mood, and seemed to foresee my recovery.
>
> —Henry David Thoreau, *Walden*

Chapter 3:
Becoming an Alien

---

*He is outside of everything, and alien everywhere.
He is an aesthetic solitary. His beautiful, light imagination is the wing that on the autumn evening just
brushes the dusky window.*

—Henry James

Aliens.
Space aliens.
Illegal aliens.

People or "beings" from another world, disconnected and
seemingly unreal.

These are common associations with the word "alien." If
we look to science fiction, aliens are usually the invaders, or
at least perceived as such. Illegal aliens are often seen as
invaders of a different sort, coming to our country to partake
of our resources. Aliens provoke interest, curiosity, and fear.
Just as in the sci-fi movies, we don't often look at things from
the alien's perspective—that is, until we find ourselves in
foreign territory. It is then that we comprehend the feelings

of vulnerability, confusion, and displacement that mark the alien experience.

Alienation is a psychological term for, simply, feeling like an alien—disconnected, weird, unreal. Diagnostically, alienation is associated with a number of psychiatric conditions, including depression, paranoia, and various personality disorders. Alienation is different than aloneness. People can be alone and still feel connected—a particular talent of introverts.

Alienation happens in society when an individual does not feel *recognized*. According to Jessica Benjamin, psychoanalyst and author of *The Bonds of Love*, "Recognition is that response from the other which makes meaningful the feelings, intentions, and actions of the self. It allows the self to realize its agency and authorship in a tangible way." Recognition is what you feel when a friend sums up exactly what you're feeling, when an author gives you the right words, when someone "gets" you.

From infancy, people serve as mirrors, reflecting back a clearer image of who we are. A baby develops a concept of self as parents instinctually mimic and respond to her. I still smile at the image of my baby in his high chair, delighted as he watched an entire table of aunts and uncles pound on the table in response to his gentle pounding on his tray. What power! As developmental theorists have observed, deprivation of early empathic mirroring can result in a range of psychological problems.

Even when we get the best parenting (and have genetics on our side) and enter the world with a strong sense of self, we don't stop using mirrors. As adults, we feel empowered and understood when we see our values reflected in society.

In an extroverted society, we rarely see ourselves in the mirror. We get alienating feedback. Alienating feedback comes in the form of repeated encouragement to join or talk, puzzled expressions, well-intended concern, and sometimes, all-out pointing and laughing. Alienating feedback happens when we hear statements like, "What kind of loser would be home on a Saturday night?" Alienating feedback happens where neighborhoods, schools, and offices provide no place to retreat. Alienating feedback happens when our quiet spaces and wilderness sanctuaries are seen as places to colonize.

ALIEN SOCIETY OR ALIEN SELF?

When an introvert looks at society and sees no reflection, she risks becoming alienated, either by staying true to herself and becoming alienated from society—called *social alienation*—or by adapting to society and becoming alienated from herself—*self-alienation.*

Some introverts accept and even embrace alienation from society, and to the extent possible, drop out of the mainstream. These are the **Shadow Dwellers,** and whether they just keep a low profile or become openly hostile to the mainstream, you probably won't be seeing many of them at a "meet and greet" function. Shadow Dwellers often feel misunderstood and different, and may see the extroverted world as hostile and inhospitable (like how I felt during kindergarten recess). At the extreme end of this continuum, a healthy introvert may become a powerful activist, whereas a psychologically—or societally—impaired introvert might become consumed by paranoia and hatred.

Another too common response is to side with culture and to turn on ourselves, asking, "Why can't I just want what everyone else wants?" The **Socially Accessible** introvert looks like an extrovert on the outside and sees extroversion as a bar that he or she can never quite reach. These individuals are often very successful in social arenas, but fault themselves for not having more fun. This self-alienation is rampant among American introverts, as is the self-interrogation—society's puzzled attitude turned inward. Alienation from self can lead to depression, which is, at best, a loss of empathy for the self and, at its worst, self-hatred. Let's look at the many introverts we don't see—either because they are in the shadows or passing as extroverts.

> *Won't you miss me? Won't you miss me at all?*
>
> —Syd Barrett, Shadow Dweller and founder of Pink Floyd, from "Dark Globe"

SHADOW DWELLERS: GOTHS, GEEKS, AND FANTASY FREAKS

Shadow Dwellers are the introverts that appear (if they can be seen) as reclusive and inaccessible—alien. These introverts often find their reflection in alternative communities or pursuits. "Goths," serious gamers, reclusive artists, writers, musicians, filmmakers, computer geeks, and fans of sci-fi, fantasy, and *anime*—to mention a few—are compelled by the inner life of the mind and the imagination. It is this quality that unites an "introvert subculture," even though individual members can be extroverted as well as introverted.

> *I am very much an introverted person. It's one of the main reasons why I wore so much black clothing during Jr. High and High School. The more I could make people afraid of me without even speaking to them, the more likely they were to not bother me.*
>
> *—JJ, artist, graphic designer, and former Goth*

If there were an archetype for the Shadow Dweller, he might take the form of a Goth. Goths are all about what's under the surface—yes, including death. An often-misunderstood group, the Goth subculture grew out of the Punk Rock movement of the late '70s. If Punk was the angry, extroverted side of anti-establishment, Goth was the sad, introverted counterpart. Most of us know Goths as those white-faced, red-lipped, black-shrouded kids who hang together and look depressed. What is easily overlooked about the seemingly death-obsessed Goths is that they are communicating an important message to society.

These "aliens" regard non-Goth people as "mundanes" (not to be confused with the "muggles" of Harry Potter's world). The Goth message to the mundanes is captured in the humanizing and often humorous book *What is Goth?* written by Goth author/artist/musician Voltaire:

> The underlying philosophy of Goth is that our society is predominantly hypocritical. Goths hold that the

"normal," "upstanding" members of our society who pretend to be "good" all of the time are in fact quite capable of doing evil. This is because Goths are often people who were victims of some kind of abuse—physical, verbal, or emotional—at the hands of these very same self-righteous folk…While Goths wear their spookiness on the outside and are largely harmless on the inside, mundanes keep their creepiness hidden, employing their socially acceptable pretenses as a disguise.

Goth philosophy reverberates with the theories of Carl Jung. According to Jung, all of the parts of ourselves that we reject go into the unconscious in the form of the Shadow archetype, while the parts we approve of become our face to the world, the Persona. If the persona is squeaky clean, the shadow will be pretty dirty. The more the shadow is denied, the more destructive its potential. On the other hand, an individual with a negative persona will have what Jung called the "white shadow." The cloistered, mild-mannered person we often find under the intimidating Goth persona is an apt example of the white shadow.

As Goth literature notes, the athletic, extroverted all-American is the accepted persona in American culture. If extroversion is the persona, introversion is the rejected, split-off shadow. And the Goth is its most dramatic spokesperson.

Goth is one of many introvert subcultures that share a preference for black, although there is a very colorful side of introvert subculture as well. Take, for example, the devoted fans of eye-popping, fanciful Japanese *anime* (animation) and *manga* (comics). This group captures the "preference for subjectivity" side of introversion that Jung also emphasized. When characters in these cartoons cry, a wild spray of water gushes from their eyes. When they are surprised, their already oversized hair shoots up in all directions. Though these fantastic images grab our attention, the genres actually encompass a broad range of themes, including science fiction, spirituality, mythology, horror, political commentary, and sometimes erotica, and are generally more psychologically sophisticated than American cartoons and comics. And if you've seen Hayao Miyazaki's Oscar-winning *Spirited Away* (2003, Best Animated Feature), you know the exquisite beauty these art forms can produce.

The phenomenal success of anime and manga in the U.S. may soon disqualify the genre from subculture status. Since 1995, when *Pokemon* was the new kid on the block, anime has become a staple of kid's television. And, as in Japan, manga is attracting American adults as well as kids. According to a Borders Books report in September 2007, manga is worth about $200 million in the U.S. alone. The paperback-style comics that read from back to front now occupy their own—very large—section in bookstores. According to Paul Gravett, author of *Manga: Sixty Years of Japanese Comics,* the word *manga* was originally employed by a Japanese print artist to describe the "looser, unself-conscious sketches in which he could play with exaggeration." Manga publishers regularly cycle in new talent to keep the sketches fresh. For a corn-fed American, the images come off as stark and often disturbing. The impact of these wild renditions on Americans perhaps parallels the way Impressionist art initially startled the refined French palate. Gravett notes that the cinematic quality of manga gives it a similar appeal to what Americans feel for movies.

> "I think I like the offensive sayings [on T-shirts] for the same reason I had my dreads, to get a rise out of people, or separate myself from the norm. To show I don't care what they think. I'm not afraid."
>
> —Ben, who lists his values as "My music career, friends, family, being a good person"

Just as geek has become chic, and we look to computer introverts with a new respect—especially if he's the CEO of our company—society can no longer ignore the human need for fantasy —if only because it *sells.* As evidenced by the astronomical prices paid for Star Trek memorabilia at an October

2006 Christie's auction, the indulgence in fantasy is no longer child's play:

> A spokesman for Christie's was quoted by *Wired* as saying, "Holy cow, we had no idea people were going to shell out that much for this plastic crap. When TV Guide started doing multiple covers with Star Trek characters years ago, I thought they were nuts! 'Who's going to buy multiple copies of TV Guide?' I thought. Well, now I know. Insane rich geeks."

Role-playing is common to many introvert subcultures, allowing the introvert to indulge in another reality and at the same time enjoy the privacy ensured by the false exterior. Acting offers a similar combination of protection and indulgence. Seeing the number of people waiting in costume to snatch the next Harry Potter book, fighting in online battles as Orcs, Ogres, and Goblins in the wildly popular *World of Warcraft,* or picking up the next manga in a favorite series, today's Spock may advise, "Pay attention and prosper."

Reclusive introverts of all sorts—whether they spend their time writing songs, programming computers, or attending sci-fi conventions—carry the paradox of looking closed off even as they open up new frontiers of the imagination. Their gifts may only be available to those who shed a little American persona and chance to visit another world.

It's important to note that not every introvert is inclined toward fantasy. Inner life means different things to different introverts. Some introverts have a strong preference for concrete rules and facts, and some prefer logical thought to the analysis of feelings. Yet, introverts tend to draw these rules, facts, or logical thoughts from an internal, subjective source—an inner form or idea or theory. In his book, *Psychological Types,* Jung said of the introverted "thinking type" (vs. the "feeling

> Be nice to nerds. Chances are you'll end up working for one.
>
> —Bill Gates, ranked the richest person in the world by *Forbes*, 1995–2007

type"), "External facts are not the aim and origin of this thinking, though the introvert would often like to make his thinking appear so." Jung was extremely critical of the Western bias toward objectivity and the need we often feel to justify our inner knowledge through external evidence. It is interesting to note that, when Isabel Briggs Myers sent him her first draft of the MBTI®, he congratulated her, but passed on her invitation to take the test. He trusted what he knew to be true.

Jung's emphasis on the subjective orientation of introverts reminds us that we are all, to some degree, Shadow Dwellers: our reference point is from within and, in this sense, we walk alone.

NO PLACE TO HIDE: THE ACCESSIBLE INTROVERT

In contrast to the Shadow Dweller, the Accessible Introvert does not come off as remote or intimidating. In fact, these introverts may be hard to distinguish from extroverts—unless you pay attention.

While I was more remote as a child, hiding in my room, writing and illustrating science fiction "books," and biting my lower lip in photos, my adult persona smiles confidently at the camera and makes inviting eye contact in conversations. I have matured into a professional who is friendly, pleasant, and approachable. And it's a problem.

While Accessible Introverts are not as subject to ridicule and social alienation, we sometimes envy Shadow Dwellers, who suffer much less intrusion, interruption, and, well, extroversion. Don't get me wrong—we like people. We just like them one or two at a time, with space in between.

Accessible Introverts are often cause-oriented people who are well trained in negotiating the social arena. The time they spend thinking about the big picture moves them to want to do something about it. Yet, they prefer the thinking to the schmoozing often required to achieve change. These accessible types also tend to identify with people who have been snubbed or teased, so they strive to be friendly to everyone. They are the kids in school who are friends with geeks and jocks alike—and secretly prefer the geeks. But the openness they put out is not entirely honest, just as the angry façade of a Shadow Dweller does not tell the whole story.

I have actually asked less-accessible friends of mine how I can put up a shield when I need more privacy. I was recently given a clue. I agreed to be photographed by an artist friend of mine, Mark Wolfe, for an exhibit he called "Faces." He was purposely mysterious about it (he's a Shadow Dweller, artist-in-black type), only telling me to dress simply with no makeup and then just look at him—no pose. I had suffered a migraine that morning, and between that and the medication I used, I was in a very internal, slowed-down state. I looked up at him, doing nothing to mask my condition. Note the difference between his "naked" photo of me and my posed press photo.

When I attended the exhibit, I was shocked by what I saw. The sad part is that I hardly recognized that face. Here are Wolfe's comments on the piece and on his *Faces* exhibit:

> As opposed to the normal face exposed to the world, I photographed my subjects with high contrast imagery devoid of make-up and soft lighting. Laurie is vivacious and energetic, always smiling…I tried to capture her "less exposed" side. All of us, especially introverts, often try to hide, disguise, or cover up ourselves. But I've found that, especially in introverts, there's a rich character that can be revealed through art. Laurie's photo is a small reflection of the inner side of a contemplative woman, exposing a deeper sensitivity and vulnerability.

Some exhibit attendees saw my image as "determined," others as "sad," still others as "thoughtful." My husband found it to be intimidating. Now that was a compliment! I recall a statement I received from my graduate school advisor, "You

© Mark Wolfe Design

could never be intimidating, Laurie." His comment—however well-intentioned—still pisses me off.

Accessible Introverts need to be pissed off more often or to tell others (nonverbally, of course) to piss off more often. We get harassed by strangers, hounded by competitors, and asked intrusive questions. We have the fatal combination of being accessible, yet lacking the extroverted capacity for comebacks. We are the ones that take a dig, mull it over, and spend days developing better and better comebacks. We can take our anger in and turn it on ourselves with demeaning self-talk, such as: "Why do you have to be such a wimp?," "Why do you let people treat you that way?," "Why didn't you say anything?" and so on.

Steve Payne Photography

Negative self-talk is a particular risk for the Accessible Introvert. Because we have *almost* adapted to the extrovert culture, we get down on ourselves for not being *more* extroverted. We look in the mirror with puzzled expressions and worry about our capacities. Sound familiar?

THE SET UP

I didn't plan on writing this section, perhaps because the topic is a painful one. But last night I had a dream that wrote it for me:

I return to my first school—the school that intimidated me as a child—for a reunion. In the large auditorium, I see Popular Girl, Insecure Girl, Tomboy Girl, and other classmates, as well as some

> Most people don't know that I'm an introvert, because I think I can fake it really, really well. At my current job, we get wined and dined a lot by drug reps, and half the time we get lunch from one of them. I love the free lunches, but it also means no "alone break" for the entire day. And the dinners and happy hours? I've gone a few times and had a lot of fun, but it takes a team of mules to get me to go.
>
> —Margit, too-accessible nurse and mom

new faces from more recent classes. Insecure Girl, who used to hang out with me—in real life we created secret codes together—greets me and excitedly tells me that I get to be one of the Homecoming Queen Contestants. The fact that she is a contestant leaves me a little suspicious, but I notice that some of the prettier and more popular girls are also contestants. I meet up with other classmates, surprised by how friendly and welcoming everyone is, including Popular Girl. (Oddly, Popular Girl is not *a contestant for Homecoming Queen.) I am also surprised, and moved, by my encounter with Tomboy Girl—my relationship with her had been lukewarm. She greets me with genuine affection and says she wants to talk to me. My extroverted little sister is there as well, loving and loyal as always.*

Much to my relief, the other contestants are putting on "uniforms" provided by the school—showgirl-like tuxedo tails over a bodysuit and tights. There are slight variations in the outfits, and I am offered one I like, with a sheer, soft blue skirt descending from the tails. I put it on in preparation for the Homecoming Parade, and as I feel all the love and attention around me, I become quite confident that I will win.

It is at this point that Popular Girl and Insecure Girl come to me with buckets of water and throw the water on my face. Everyone laughs, and I soon realize that I have been set up. The whole invitation, the confidence building—everything had been designed for this punch line. This humiliation.

I run out in tears, then angrily return to grab my clothes. I am struck that nobody expresses regret or tries to get me to stay. They are still laughing and enjoying the gag. I see a book titled "The Children," and the last page is closing, suggesting that this is the end of the story, the resolution of the plot.

THE COURAGE TO BE ALONE

Though the taboo against solitude presses against us, half of the population continues to declare our *preference* for introversion. It may take awhile, but introverts eventually catch a reflection and like what they see. And despite criticism within and without, we find ways to be alone. Whether we find solitude in the woods or in the anonymity of the city, in a library or a monastery, or simply in the comfort of home, we find it. And when we finally calm the din of fearful chatter and, with Whitman "inhale great draughts of space," we can declare with the poet:

> *I am larger, better than I thought,*
> *I did not know I held so much goodness.*

I feel despair as I consider the options: Leave and be forgotten, or return and "take the joke." I do start to return, but with a third option in mind...

The dilemma I was left with in the dream is *The Dilemma* of the introvert: to disappear or to play along. The prospect of popularity had enticed Insecure Girl to betray me—a former ally—and likewise seduced me into participating in the popularity contest. Even as I walk away, broken, the power of popularity prevents anyone from reaching out to me. [Note: my husband read this and informed me that my dream was almost an exact replay of the '70s horror flick *Carrie*—except that the classmates poured pig's blood over her and then she started killing people. I had purposely missed that movie. Perhaps the theme is archetypal.]

Just before I wake up, I consider a third option—to ignore the groupthink and talk to people separately. I was drawn to Tomboy Girl, who I knew I could trust, and to my loving sister. Somehow, I knew I had real friends amid the laughing crowd, and I decided to find recognition in them.

THE THIRD OPTION

The third option, for Shadow Dwellers and Accessible Introverts alike, is to know you have friends—and to be a friend. It is easy for the many of us to sacrifice the few: to allow the Goth or the Geek to take the rap, while secretly sharing their passion for the intricate contents of the mind. I used to write science fiction stories that stunned by literary mother. I had vivid, and sometimes terrifying, dreams at night. My older sister said that, when I was daydreaming, I seemed to enter a trancelike state. I am still convinced that, when I was little, I *floated* down the stairs every morning.

But I now know that I'm not that unusual. We all have our introverted little secrets. I recall attending a lecture on dreams, and feeling immense relief when the speaker described people like me as "ideationally gifted." "Yes! That's me," I thought.

"Not crazy or weird, but *ideationally gifted.*" As introverts, we have a greater tolerance for the contents of the mind. Some of us see into other worlds; some of us see inside patterns and equations; some of us access spiritual truths. But if any of us are weird, we all are. We were manga when manga wasn't cool.

Most of us also carry our stories of humiliation. And, sadly, many of us, like Insecure Girl in my dream, have participated in the humiliation of other introverts—introverts who were unable or unwilling to participate in the extroverted games.

As you start to challenge the extrovert assumption and reclaim the gift of your inner life, don't be surprised if you encounter feelings of grief or anger. Introverts have a habit of becoming admirably hip as we find vehicles for our gifts, but we also know the pain of being teased, laughed at, and left out—even if we only experience the ridicule indirectly, through a more honest member of our group.

As Gloria Steinem said, "The truth will set you free. But first, it will piss you off."

Chapter 4:
"Anyone Else IN?"

Loneliness is proof that your innate search for connection is intact.

—Martha Beck

Half of us.

More than half of us prefer introversion to extroversion.

When I share this fact with introverts, they consistently react with disbelief. Half. I almost have to say it as a mantra to myself, because I also have been programmed to believe that our numbers are few. But the assumption that introverts are the exception is not just something floating around in the ether; it's available in any bookstore. Virtually every self-help book on introversion to date indicates that we make up one-third of the population. One of these, hot off the press in 2007, states: "They [extroverts] represent the norm of Western society and outnumber introverts three to one."

If you search the Internet, as introverts often do, some sources estimate that introverts make up only *one-fourth* of the population. A 2004 "Ask Yahoo" entry posed the question, "What's the ratio of introverts to extroverts in the human population?" The response? "According to several sources, extroverts make up 60 to 75 percent of the population." And "several sources" *do* place introverts in the minority—confidently, conclusively. The belief in the minority status of introverts has seeped into our pores and become conventional wisdom.

In order to get a perspective on how this happened, we'll need to rewind about fifty years. Bear with me: you need to see it to believe it.

A vast amount of data is generated from the Myers-Briggs Type Indicator (MBTI®), which is available in twenty-one languages and is administered to over two million individuals each year. The MBTI® measures introversion and extroversion, along with the other aspects of type developed by Jung and his successors.

During the formative stages of the MBTI®, beginning in 1942 and resulting in the first *MBTI® Manual* in 1962, Isabel Briggs Myers realized that she needed to get a read on the percentages of introverts and extroverts in the population. This was not an easy task at the time. Population studies were extremely rare, and would have been unheard of for a test instrument. Myers still was not satisfied to rely on her hunches, so she carefully designed and conducted a study of 399 male eleventh and twelfth grade students. Only 26.9 percent of the boys were identified as introverted. Myers adjusted the percentage to correct for the bias of her sample, and came up with her population estimate of "one-third." The estimate was published in the 1962 manual, though the study supporting it was never published.

It is important to note that the MBTI® is not a static entity. In the tradition established by Myers herself, the test continued to be "tested" with progressively larger samples. What started as Form A is now Form M, and by my count, the MBTI® has undergone a good ten revisions—and counting! This progressive tradition has spawned a vast amount of research over the years. But in 1998, researchers were finally able to do what Isabel Briggs Myers could not: an actual population study. The study was based on a national *representative* sample—3,009 randomly selected individuals—which, through weighting of underrepresented groups, was made to approximate the distribution of the 1990 U.S. Census. The findings were clear: introverts and extroverts are equally represented in the population. A follow-up study, using a national representative sample of 1,378 subjects, was published in 2001. The new study not only dispels the myth of an extrovert majority, but turns it upside-down: introverts represent 57 percent of the population, and extroverts trail behind at 43 percent. The estimate made over forty years earlier has been rendered obsolete.

Or so it would seem.

Why is the outdated minority statistic referenced so often? One reason may be the tendency to use secondary references in publications. Isabel Briggs Myers used her original estimate in her book, *Gifts Differing*, first published in 1980. When the popular book was printed again in 1995, the chapter on introversion and extroversion still quoted the statistic, though a footnote clarifies, "An early, unpublished study by Isabel Briggs Myers is the basis of statements in this chapter about the frequencies of types in the general population." Other authors quoted this statistic without the footnote, and their books became references to other sources. Before long, "several sources" were repeating Myers' original estimate, and a fact was born. What seemed to be several was actually one well-reasoned but extremely out-of-date statistic.

Another problem may be the complexity of MBTI® data. Introversion is often embedded within more specific personality types, represented in codes such as ISTJ or IFTP. Yet, the percentages of introversion and extroversion are often noted separately or can be obtained by adding up the results for the eight introvert types.

What puzzled me in my own research is that it was actually very *difficult* for me to figure out where the much-quoted 1:3 ratio came from. The authoritative clearinghouse for MBTI® data is available in the *MBTI® Manual*, which, at this writing, is in the second printing of its third edition. Because the current research didn't support the ratio, I started working my way backward in the thick manual, first hitting on results from an earlier national representative study: "In the 1996 sample, Introverts were slightly more common [than extroverts] for both genders." No help there. Though I read about numerous studies, I saw nothing to suggest that introverts were in the minority. I eventually abandoned the "thick manual," and continued to search for the elusive data—until I found Myers' footnote in the back of her book.

Our ability to overlook the *three* editions of accumulated data on introversion and extroversion, spanning a period of over fifty years, and to at least not *equivocate* about the applicability of the original estimate, is quite remarkable. Maybe the truth got lost in translation from the academic to popular literature, but perhaps something less conscious and more insidious is at work.

Sometimes it takes an observation from outside our culture to see what is too close to identify. The *MBTI® Manual* reiterates an anecdote shared by attendees at a "psychological type" conference in Great Britain: The U.S. attendees found it hard to identify the extroverts among their British colleagues because they did not act like American extroverts. The British attendees reported a similar difficulty identifying introverts in America because "U.S. Introverts exhibited behavior that in the United Kingdom was associated with Extroversion: sociability, comfort with small talk, disclosure of personal information, energetic and fast-paced conversation, and so forth." Most Americans, whether introverted or extroverted, have learned to look like extroverts.

It's one thing if extroverts don't see us, but it's even more tragic when introverts no longer see introverts. It's a chicken-egg problem: if there are so few of us, why look? If we don't look, we don't see. But does it matter? After all, we like being alone. Correction: we like being *introverted.* Yes, we do have the need for solitude, and we enjoy time alone, but we also like to be introverted in more public settings, and we relate in our own way. We enjoy a different conversational pace than extroverts, namely, one that allows people to think. We are moved by ideas, and make connections through shared interests. We love the

comfort of hanging out when there's no pressure to talk. *Half.*
More than half of us.

When we stop seeing introverts, we not only feel alienated,
but we lose power. We don't like competing anyway, but if there
are just a handful of us, it's just easier to adapt. The assumption
of extroversion can prevent us from taking the risk—when it
may not be that risky after all—of being openly introverted. And
when we adapt and either pass as extroverts or stay on the sidelines, the extrovert assumption is strengthened and our power
further erodes. Let's look a little closer at what we're assuming.

THE EXTROVERSION ASSUMPTION

As we grow and adapt to American society, we internalize the
assumption that extroversion is normal and introversion is a
deviation. Here's a quick sampling of some of the messages we
take in:

- Parties are fun
- Being popular is important
- It's "who you know"
- Networking is essential to success
- It's not good to be alone
- It's important to be a "team player"
- Most people are extroverts
- The more the merrier

If we assume that everyone around us is extroverted, as our
society leads us to believe, we naturally feel less comfortable in
public settings. We may feel that we need to keep our introverted ways to ourselves and adapt while among people. We
don't even pause to think that others might also crave a deeper
conversation and a quieter room. When we go to an obligatory
party, we assume that everyone else wants to be there. After all,
"parties are fun!" Rest assured, any party with an obligatory
component has invitees who are wishing they were elsewhere,
along with some who have managed to *be* elsewhere.

In the American workplace, introverts often feel immense pressure to be extroverted. Whether spoken or not, we pick up the assumption that we're supposed to make friends at work. Introverts don't get this. We generally go to work to *work*. I can hear the protest, "But it's more fun to have friends at work!" Here is another extrovert assumption. Extroverts are energized through interaction. They are happy to create more friendships, because then there are more people to keep the interactions going—after work, on the weekend, at parties, and so on.

Introverts more often see the workplace as a place to interact with *ideas*. A friendly greeting is fine and good, but workplace chatter feels distracting and intrusive. And if we work with clients or customers, we may be all the more protective of our social energies. Yet, the extrovert assumption is so woven into the fabric of our culture that an employee may suffer reprimands for keeping his door closed (that is, if he is one of the lucky ones who *has* a door), for not lunching with other staff members, or for missing the weekend golf game or any number of supposedly morale-boosting celebrations. *Half. More than half* of us don't want to play. We don't see the point. For us, an office potluck will not provide satisfying human contact—we'd much rather meet a friend for an intimate conversation (even if that friend is a coworker). For us, the gathering will not boost morale — and will probably leave us resentful that we stayed an extra hour to eat stale cookies and make small talk. For us, talking with coworkers does not benefit our work—it sidetracks us.

Whether we are at work or at play, the extrovert assumption prevails and alienates over half of the population. *Half.* Not just a few nerdy recluses, but more than half of us.

FINDING INTROVERTS

Whether we want to make a new friend or not, it is crucial that we start to see "the other half" of the population. Just knowing our numbers—solid numbers that have been available for a decade but have yet to be *known*—changes our perceptions. It is very hard to argue that over half of the population is weird or somehow deviant. Be clear—we don't have to gather or, heaven forbid, have a big party to be strengthened by our numbers. We just need to know the truth.

But it does help to *see* as well. And once you know there are more like you out there, you'll notice things—like the fact that coffeehouses have popped up everywhere. Coffeehouses! Places where people read or write or draw or just chill. Quiet places. At this moment, I happen to be typing at a coffeehouse inside a large bookstore. There are eleven other people scattered among the tables and couches—even a little family with mom, dad, a little boy, and a baby—and *no one* is talking! I keep waiting for voices, and all I hear is the soothing background music. I am the most impressed by the family: the baby is sucking on a rattle; the boy eats his ice cream and then studies the scene outside the window; mom and dad read. When the boy eventually asks a question, the parents respond to him quietly, and when the baby starts to fuss, they get up and exit as if to leave the sleeping undisturbed.

But on their way out, an observer makes a comment about the baby and continues to deliver a monologue to the couple, loudly—a bull in a china shop. The young parents are clearly uncomfortable, and politely break away as quickly as possible. This place operates under the assumption of introversion. Most of the inhabitants are by themselves, and tables are small to accommodate intimate conversation, if necessary.

I have noticed that, when larger groups meet in a coffeehouse, they usually have something to *do,* such as reading and critiquing each other's writing, planning an event, reviewing the movie they just attended, or sharing a side-by-side activity such as knitting. It is a culture of ideas, and extroverts seeking a place to meet, greet, and mingle soon get bored and leave.

It is no secret that these introvert enclaves are amazingly successful, and the reason is as easily apparent. *Half. More than half* of us now have a place to be publicly introverted. You think it's the coffee? The people who primarily want the coffee take it

> I often do seek out places where I can do something solitary (reading, drawing, writing, handwork) but among other people, like coffee houses, cafes, or the library. I see a lot of people doing more of this now, and it makes me feel good, reassured that I'm not alone in my craving for time with myself without the necessity of conversation but in the presence of humans doing the same.
>
> —Suzanne, who would like extroverts to know, "We're OKAY being introverts, and, no, we don't wish we could be just like them."

to go. As I scan the room, only one of the eleven is drinking coffee—at least I *think* it's coffee: some dark blended drink topped with loads of whipped cream and chocolate syrup. Maybe that person, like me, sees the purchase as a very reasonable rent payment on some prime introvert real estate.

But let's say you're at a social event. Finding the introverts in this setting requires a bit more skill. You may find one or two on the fringes of the activity or outside getting air. Some will be locked in a group conversation, but you can tell they aren't really present—they keep glancing at their watch or the door. Unfortunately, many introverts are pros at holding a look of interest while most of their focus is directed inward. The best indicators of introversion are very subtle: a concentrating expression, a tendency to look off at nothing in particular—indicators that the person is thinking. These are the kind of hard-to-define expressions that artists love to capture in portraits.

Still others will be cloistered with a spouse or close friend, talking in hushed tones to signal to others, "this is private." The introverts generally leave early, energy drained, while the most extroverted gain momentum and stay until the end—and then are ready for the "after party."

A New Assumption

Though common wisdom would suggest that introverts should connect by starting a conversation, we are discovering that common wisdom is not very trustworthy when it comes to introverts. Introverts work from the inside out, and the simplest and most profound way that we can connect is by *acting like introverts.* And we will feel freer to act like introverts when we know that others—many others—get it.

Start by carrying around the 57 percent statistic as you go about your day. As you look around you, keep in mind that more than half of us are introverted—half of the people in your neighborhood, half of the people downtown, half of the people on campus. When I was little, I got scared if I was awake while everyone else in the house was sleeping. I learned to comfort myself by remembering that there were other people awake, even though I couldn't see them: night shift workers, people flying to different countries, telephone operators. There is something powerful in knowing that you are not the only one holding up a certain kind of consciousness—the only one awake. Even if you can't see the others, knowing they are there helps.

Buoyed by the comfort of knowing that you have quiet, like-minded company, you can relax into your introversion. You can bring your power source with you. Perhaps you can even meditate—right in the middle of that big old mosh pit called America.

WHERE THE (INNER) ACTION IS

Perhaps the biggest challenge is to see other introverts when they are alone. I was recently watching the remarkable BBC video series "Planet Earth." I was able to view the rare snow leopard in its natural habitat, thanks to the solitary watch of the cameraman camping in the remote mountains of Pakistan. As I observed these speckled, sphinx-like inhabitants of the snowy mountains, I felt gratitude for the photographers who embraced solitude—one was on a three-year assignment—in order to bring me this vision.

Even introverts—you'd think we would know better—are prone to see the solitary introvert in a very flat and limited way: usually gaunt white guy, often in front of a computer, low in energy, malnourished, bored and stuck in some kind of repetitive activity or inactivity. When forming impressions, it is quite American to skim the surface, to surf and schmooze and sample. But to know the introvert, surfing won't do. If I had only seen the solitary cameraman in his hut, looking through his lens—there was some footage of this—I would have become quickly bored. But beholding *what he was seeing* gave me chills.

Let's go to Zurich, Switzerland, circa 1914, to observe another solitary soul. This man is a respected scholar who has abandoned his teaching at the university, because he doesn't want to continue teaching until he's figured some things out. He continues to see patients and attend to his family, but spends vast stretches of time alone, reclining and staring off into space, occasionally scribbling some notes. If we look just at the face of it, we may wonder why he's withdrawing, why he traded a prestigious position for this sitting around. We might be concerned that he's become socially phobic or depressed—or both.

This rising intellect was Carl Jung, and he was conducting an experiment, using himself as the sole subject. He used a process similar to self-hypnosis to submerge himself deeper and deeper into the unconscious, the part of the mind where dreams and fantasies live. His methods and discoveries are chronicled in his fascinating biography, *Memories, Dreams, Reflections.*

As a diver going beneath the calm surface of the ocean, Jung found a world teeming with life. He discovered what he called the "collective unconscious," a reality beyond the level of the personal unconscious that emerges through universal symbols and products of culture, from art to mythology. He even found a cast of characters—*archetypes*—Great Mother, Hero, Trickster, and the infamous Shadow, to name just a small sample.

For an introvert, a placid surface may be evidence that the introvert, to borrow Adrienne Rich's words, "has moved on, deeper into the heart of the matter." As with Jung, the exterior of inactivity may belie a vast internal wonderland. Seeing the introverts who are out of sight, and getting a glimpse of worlds they inhabit, asks more of us than a simple introduction.

Seeing an introvert means knowing there's more. It means looking for her ideas, her observations, her creations. Introverts talk to us every day through their stories, theories, movies, technology, paintings, songs, inventions—the list is endless. For the introvert, conversation can be a very limited forum for self-expression. When a song moves you, a writer "gets" you, or a theory enlightens you—you and its creator are connecting in a realm beyond sight or speech. Not all of these expressions come from introverts, nor does every introvert's idea reach a wider audience. But connecting through the contents of the mind is the introvert's way.

> *This comparison [the introvert stereotype versus the real me] just shows me how complicated people are, and that they can appear like an introvert on the outside but every day surround themselves with wonder and mystery.*
>
> —Solveig, high school sophomore, who enjoys thinking and drawing in her room

You might take the time to find out who took the photo you so admire in a magazine; by the way, the photographers I viewed on watch (at different locations) for snow leopards were Doug Allen and Mark Smith. When you are stunned by what your cell phone can do, consider the person who designed the tiny circuitry. Start humanizing the ideas you hold and hear and read and see every day. And when you want to meet an introvert, try asking what the person is thinking or observing. A great question someone once asked me was, "How do you like to express yourself?" Reach beyond the surface.

MY SPACE IN CYBERSPACE

In cyberspace, the rules of engagement favor introverts. We can connect while remaining alone. We can read and write rather than talk. And we can more comfortably network with people who share our interests and ideas. Like the coffeehouse, cyberspace allows introverts to be alone more publicly. Introverts can post profiles, blogs, and videos without seeking an agent or a publisher. We can create or join communities based on even our quirkiest ideas. We can connect with other introverts enjoying the same playground. And we can turn it off whenever we want.

The computer is my introverted but sometimes intimate connection to the world of my choosing.

—Don, passionate about baseball, music, politics, religion, exercise, and the author's sister

This worried comment inevitably arises: "But that's no substitute for *real* relationships!" This concern makes sense if we're comparing an Internet chat to a sustained relationship with a partner or close friend. And it is true that an Internet user can invent a personality online. There is more freedom on the Internet, for better *and* for worse. But just as the Internet may limit relationships, it can also create, expand, and enrich them. Online dating is a godsend for many introverts who cringe at the idea of meeting someone at a bar or social event. Where else but cyberspace does the introvert have the opportunity to *start* in our comfort zone of written communication and talk later? How else can you defy geography and search widely for a soul connection? And because introverts can often open up more easily in a written message, Internet communication can also enhance existing relationships.

Though computerized communications may seem cold, the fact is, we're *writing* again—we're even writing with our phones! Though I still prefer the art of letter writing, it is an infrequent luxury. An email or text message offers a similar indulgence without the hassle.

Unless you're talking about sex, I'm not so sure that live is always better. It is part of the extrovert assumption to value interaction over *inner* action. Most introverts savor live time with a close friend, because they know there will be plenty of inner action for both of them. But much of what we call "social" in America allows for very little inner action. Emailing a friend or posting a blog entry will probably feel much richer, and help us feel much closer, than being up close and impersonal.

Chapter 5: Meditating with the Majority: The Introverted Society

The first great thing is to find yourself and for that you need solitude and contemplation—at least sometimes. I can tell you deliverance will not come from the rushing noisy centers of civilization. It will come from the lonely places.

—Fridtjof Nansen

Everywhere we looked in Japan, we saw calm and order.

—T. R. Reid

I recently watched a television interview of a woman who had been born into a cult. Having no other reality to judge hers against, she discussed how hard it was to find validation of her feeling that things were not right. Having to marry her uncle felt creepy, but everyone around her said it was good.

This woman's circumstances brought home to me the importance of self-validation—and of introversion. The introvert's habit of keeping "one foot out" of a given social grouping—whether it be family, community, or society—is a lifesaver, sometimes *literally*, when the group stifles or oppresses what the individual values.

As I look back, I kept one foot out of most places I inhabited. Since my formative years in rural Minnesota, I have taken up residence in various parts of the country, from the Rockies and the Sierra Nevadas, to East Coast cities, and on to my current home nestled in an Appalachian river city. Being somewhat of a vagabond—to the extent you can be one while getting married and raising children—I have made a hobby of studying the psychological nuances of culture. What I now also realize is that I've been looking for my home—a home that allows me to practice, rather than defend, my introversion; to, perhaps, allow both feet to rest inside. Like Goldilocks in the story of "The Three Bears," I have been looking for a place to sit down that is just right— the place that feels comfortable and allows me to relax into who I am.

Searching for home helps us define what it is we need. It wasn't until I left Minnesota that I developed an appreciation for its introverted characteristics, and I have found different pieces of the puzzle in each place I have lived. You have likely gathered your own pieces of the puzzle, and this may be a good time to take note of your discoveries. Introverts are, by nature, travelers. Whether you use the vehicle of literature, cinema, the Internet, the open road, or the limitless sky, you have probably visited many worlds. And if you enjoy science fiction or fantasy, you are particularly adept at envisioning alternative realities. You may want to take a moment and write a list of these places, real or imagined, and identify the features of each place that help you feel comfortably introverted.

But does such an alternative reality even exist? If America is extroverted, are there other societies that are introverted? What would an introverted society look like, feel like? What are the elements of an introverted society?

Let's explore two cultures that have been identified with introversion: Nordic culture, or *Norden,* and Japan.

NORDEN: PRIVATE AND PROUD

Norden, meaning "the north," refers to the countries that make up the Nordic Council: Denmark, Finland, Iceland, Norway, and Sweden. Though each country has its own distinct character, commonalities in language and geography give it the flavor we know as "Scandinavian."

Growing up in the American North—Minnesota—gave me an early taste for Scandinavian culture. I knew my heritage. I am 100 percent Norwegian, a descendant of the Vikings. We are tough and stoic. We don't whine. Life, as my dad put it, was "sweat, blood, and tears." Like Norway, Minnesota was cold, so we had to reserve energy and be resilient. People—except, it seemed, the ones *living with me*—didn't talk more than necessary; they just took care of things.

This "Norden of the U.S." values privacy and reserve, along with a code of civility—the "Minnesota Nice" I learned so well—that engenders clean neighborhoods and respectful interactions. If your shopping cart accidentally hits someone else's, you plead "I'm sorry" (with an emphasis on the "o" sound, of course). Some grocery stores in the metro area of Minneapolis-St. Paul provide carpeted floors, chandeliers, and soft music; clean indoor air was guaranteed long before this became a national trend; and lawns, even in poorer neighborhoods, are well-tended and trimmed. Lakes within the city limits are kept clean, and are encircled by walking and bike paths, benches and parkland.

Still, Minnesotans who visit a city in the homeland, such as Bergen, Norway, are stunned by its beauty and cleanliness. Public bathrooms are immaculate, brightly colored flowers spill out of window boxes (in season), and the air is crisp and clean. Introverts are less likely to feel overstimulated here, and are spared the constant evidence (i.e., trash) of the other people who share this space. Author Donald S. Connery captures this "freshness" in his book, *The Scandinavians:*

> Norway has the clear-eyed appearance of the freshest, cleanest, and most natural nation in Europe. It is almost as if the weary and sophisticated continent had set Norway apart as a national park or royal preserve and had appointed the Norwegians as custodians to keep the waters clear, the mountain snows untouched by industrial soot, and the wonders of nature unspoiled by thoughtless trespassers.

Salivating? There's more. There's not only more natural space outside, but employees in Norden get more space at work, both for their thinking and for their time *away* from work. The prevailing form of government, social democracy, embraces consensus decision-making, a more inclusive, "feminine" style of management, and attention to the individual worker. While this may seem a far cry from the Viking way of getting things done, there's another side to that story. These brutal warriors are thought to have established the first democracy — in the form of regular common meetings. Radical for the times, women and handicapped people could attend. These meetings, translated, were called "The Thing"—all hail Scandinavian simplicity!

The value of the individual voice continues to be evident in the Norden workplace. Managers go to lengths to see that each employee is represented in decision-making, and often meet privately with individuals to solicit their views. A relative of mine who works for a Danish company said that the efforts to reach consensus in meetings were frustrating for her at first, and required her to slow down the more driven pace she had been accustomed to. The discussions foster *inner action* as well as interaction, allowing a deeper level of analysis and understanding.

And, perhaps most attractive of all for the introvert, Norden employees get an abundance of time *away* from work. While an American mother often struggles to put together even a short maternity leave—using her vacation time or unpaid family leave—a Swedish mom and dad get *over a year* of parental leave to divide up as they choose. That's *paid* leave at 80 percent of salary. The Swedes also know how to vacation—about seven weeks a year, paid, not counting holidays. The other Nordic countries also have generous policies, and members of the European Union are guaranteed at least twenty days of paid leave. The United States, which provides no minimum leave requirement, was referred to in one analysis as the "No-Vacation Nation."

So Nordic people are virtually guaranteed two resources introverts crave: space and time. The Norden personality emphasizes privacy, restraint, respect, and equality—values an introvert can appreciate. The dominantly Lutheran religious culture emphasizes private faith over public evangelism. Show-offs are *not* appreciated. Norden restraint has been the target of parodies and jokes, passed around freely in Minnesota, and often heard on Garrison Keillor's *A Prairie Home Companion*. An example: "Did you hear about the Norwegian who loved his wife so much he almost told her?"

Could we be talking about *repression* here, rather than restraint? Are these people too nice to be fun? Is there a "wild inside" under the surface? Here are some observations:

- The wild in Norway is found in nature, and in the physicality of the hardy people who live there. The mountainous country is cut by deep fjords and stunning lakes, until the landscape drops sharply to ragged coastline dotted with innumerable islands. Almost a third of the country extends north of the Arctic Circle. As author Donald Connery put it, "Norway is nature gone berserk." Introverts who would rather contend with nature than people would probably find a home here, as well as those of us who secretly enjoy being snowed in. Many Northerners resonate with the intensely private John Steinbeck, who wrote, "I've lived in a good climate, and it bores the hell out of me. I like weather rather than climate."

- The lands that produced the great existentialist Søren Kierkegaard (Denmark) and master filmmaker Ingmar Bergman (Sweden) reflect their deeply introspective characters. Geographic isolation and long, dark winters are conducive to "going inside," psychologically as well as physically. At its darkest, around December 21, northern Norway sees no day at all; the sun does not rise.
- Intellectual pursuit and creativity also thrive in Norden, and introverted thinkers find a welcoming environment. Sweden's child, Alfred Nobel, is the archetype of the generative introvert. A chemist and physicist, he is best known for inventing dynamite and for his will, which established and funded the legacy now known as the Nobel Prize—the highest honor for achievements in world peace, science, and literature. In addition to holding 350 patents and controlling factories and laboratories in twenty countries, Nobel was fluent in five languages and wrote novels, poetry, and plays in his spare time. Who has time to socialize?
- Statistics from the World Health Organization (2007) indicate that each of the five Nordic countries have higher suicide rates than the U.S.; however, a meta-analysis of life satisfaction studies (Adrian White, University of Leicester) suggest that Norden is a very happy place. Denmark ranked the happiest of the 178 nations; Iceland came in fourth (in another study, Iceland was on top), Finland and Sweden were close behind, and Norway kept Norden in the top twenty by placing 19th. The U.S. placed 23rd. White suggested that the higher rate of suicide in Norden reflects the impact of long, dark winters, not the overall quality of life. But the Nordic thinkers are on that, too: "Light cafes" allow you to sip a latte while basking in the glow of therapeutic light boxes. And the mood swings bright in this "Land of the Midnight Sun," when, around June 21, the sun stays out all night.

So, other than the weather (which, let's face it, sucks) is there a downside to this healthy, prosperous, civil, highly educated, and vacation-abundant region? The "middle way" government, with features of both democracy and socialism, seems quite suited to the introvert, who requires freedom but is not big on competition. But citizens do pay for the balance: taxes are extremely high, and an introvert building a small business may be hard pressed to pay for the extravagant leave guaranteed to its employees. As a relatively isolated and homogeneous culture, it is likely that an introvert would feel *very* at home here, or *very* trapped—that is, until that paid vacation rolls around.

JAPAN: MANNERS OVER MOUTH

As a child living in my mini-Norden, a country home next to a white-steepled Lutheran church, I developed a fascination with Japanese culture. In contrast to the monochromatic feel of a Minnesota winter, Japan was color to me—from the jewel-toned kimono of the geisha to the ornate temples that looked like something out of Disneyland. Granted, my experience of Japan *was* highly influenced by Disney World—and my fixation on the Japanese children in "It's a Small World." Indeed, mine was a small world. Still, I have a picture book in my mind of my collected Japan experiences, from visiting a Japanese tea garden in San Francisco to receiving a green silk kimono-style robe from my much-traveled aunt. As a young person, I wanted to learn Ikebana (the Japanese art of flower arranging), to raise a Bonsai (those ancient but tiny twisted trees), and to one day visit Tokyo, a place that fully met the definition of foreign to me.

If you look back, you may also have collected a culture as a child. I have yet to visit Tokyo, and had all but forgotten my childhood vow to visit—which I had put in writing, by the way—until I began the research for this book. Jung would smile: important archetypes have a way of coming back.

Japan was my archetype, but I didn't know why. Whatever it was that drew me, I felt it in the intricacies of the tea garden: the path leading through a wonderland of exquisite greenery in every texture and shape, the mossy backdrop contrasting with grey stones, accents of pink wisteria and blue iris, leading me over trickling water by way of arching miniature bridges, or alongside a pond featuring the reflection of the tiered pagoda, to a bench ready for me in the shade. If I'm getting carried away in my description, I am only capturing how I felt—carried away. I felt careful here, but in a good way, like I wanted to walk on my tiptoes and not disturb the experience. I shivered with secret delight. I didn't want to leave. Ever.

Now I realize that my experience in the tea garden captured what is introverted about Japanese society. Here was a space, created with such care, not for large gatherings or shared rituals. Here was a space designed to honor the private experience—a space that honored *me*.

If the Nordic people are respectful, the Japanese are *reverent*. The customary greeting of the bow is an example of this reverence, as is the common preface of "honorable" when addressing someone, as in "honorable customer." Even the *signs* speak the language of reverence. T. R. Reid, former Tokyo bureau chief for the *Washington Post* and author of *Confucius Lives Next Door,* quoted a sign his neighbor put up to stop cars from blocking his narrow driveway: "We're sorry, but we must respectfully request that owners of honorable cars not connected to this household cooperate by refraining from parking in front of our humble driveway."

I felt that reverence in the tea garden. Even though other people were enjoying the garden, I felt like I was the only inhabitant. The landscaping, arched bridges, and foliage seemed designed to block my view of the others. I was able to inhabit my own space in this public place.

And the Japanese know that, oftentimes, the best way to honor you is to *leave you alone*. They honor personal space, perhaps because they have always had so little of it. When Americans meet someone for the first time, we feel obliged to extend a hand and introduce ourselves. This practice is considered intrusive in Japan, where *enryo* (pronounced inn-rio), translated as "holding back" or "restraint," governs interactions.

It is common courtesy to give the other person time to size up the situation, to not overwhelm the person with your presence, so introductions are unlikely at the first meeting. Can you imagine people acting this way in America? We are taught to act on the extrovert assumption, that interaction is what people want. The Japanese seem to operate on the assumption that *space and time* are what people want—the introvert assumption. Unfortunately, we have not figured out how to import *enryo* along with Toshiba electronics and Toyota cars.

Intrusive behavior is commonplace in America. You and a friend are having an intimate conversation in the restaurant, and a friend of your friend comes right over and interrupts you to say hello and start a new conversation. You're on the freeway, a lane is closing ahead, and you dutifully move over — while others use the opportunity to move ahead of you and merge at the last minute. You're on the phone and politely say you've got to go; the person on the other end keeps talking.

While these examples are annoying, especially for us introverts, intrusion takes on a whole new meaning when it comes in the form of violence—and it's here where *we* could stand to feel some of that shame so associated with the Japanese. According to 1998 statistics from the United Nations' Office on Drugs and Crime, murders per capita were eight times more common in the U.S. than in Japan; rapes were twenty-five times more common, aggravated assault eighty-one times more common, and robbery was a staggering 146 times more common in the U.S. If you're thinking that they must have a punitive police force and scary prisons, not so. According to Reid, "the nation has one-third as many police per capita, one-fifth as many judges, one-twentieth as many jail cells" as the United States. Reid, who lived with his family in Japan for five years, set out to explain this "social miracle." His answer: Confucius.

> You cannot be an introvert and live on a cul-de-sac.
>
> —Margit, who now lives on a corner and is much happier

Confucianism, more a code of ethics than a religion, has been woven into the fabric of Japanese life since the dawn of formal education. If you want to get a real feel for this phenomenon, read *Confucius Lives Next Door,* but to employ the American "bottom line," here's the gist: *Everyone is responsible for making things work.* Harmony, or *wa,* is a central value, and responsibility for *wa* is taught right alongside reading, geography, and math. The policing body is the individual conscience—the guilt and shame we are so phobic of in America.

Here's the paradox of Japan: It's a society that honors the whole over the individual, and because of that, individuals don't get in your way. It's a traditionally vertical society with strong moral codes, but the codes apply to the owners and managers as much as they do to the workers. And what about pay? A 2001 *BusinessWeek* story reported that, while CEOs for the top U.S. companies made *531 times* as much as their employees, Japan's top CEOs make ten times more than the employees, the lowest discrepancy of all the countries surveyed. And, perhaps the biggest paradox of all, Tokyo is a bustling city of over twelve million people, yet Reid felt comfortable allowing his ten-year-old girl to go with her ten-year-old friend—by train, *by themselves*—to Tokyo Disneyland for the day.

As I read Reid's account, I became conscious of how important *safety* is to the introvert. I remembered going on a long walk while vacationing with my parents, returning happy and refreshed, only to be greeted by a lecture from mom and dad: I was a young woman, and it was dangerous for me to be walking alone in a strange place. I remember the lecture well, because my parents were not typically that protective; with ten kids, they had learned to trust our resilience. I also remember my refusal to take in what they were saying. That walk, beyond the boundaries of shared territory, elevated me to a timeless reality that I knew was good. How could this be ill-advised? My assumption of safety may have been naïve—though I did return unscathed—but it was an assumption I did not want to give up. And, apparently, it's an assumption that is alive and well in Japan.

In the way Norden attends to the mind, Japan attends to the spirit. The ancient and distinctly Japanese religion of *Shintoism* teaches that the divine spirit infuses all things, which may explain why all things are so honored in Japan, whether natural or material. The beauty and symmetry of nature are seen as reflections of the gods. The school of Buddhism called *Zen*—derived from the word "meditation"—became popular in Japan for its focus on spiritual practice rather than religious study. And, in Japan, life seems to *be* a meditation. Numerous practices, from sweeping the floor to writing calligraphy to serving tea, infuse the mundane with spiritual meaning and beauty.

Now I realize that the Japanese values of restraint, harmony, and spiritual care had all contributed to my experience in the tea garden. But what cost do the Japanese people pay for this beauty, this reverence — for their "social miracle"? While violence against others is rare, violence against the self is a problem. Japan has one of the highest suicide rates among industrialized countries—a problem that the government is finally addressing through a ten-year suicide-reduction initiative. And, even with moves toward equality, Japanese women are still affected by longstanding prohibitions against their personal fulfillment, which are often summed up as the *Three Obediences.* "When she is young, she obeys her father; when she is married, she obeys her husband; when she is widowed, she obeys her son." And much media attention has focused on the *hikikomori*—young people, usually male, who shut themselves in their rooms for at least six months, and often years. These young men often feel overwhelmed by the pressure to succeed in such a performance-oriented society; some are rebelling over their limited career options, and many have been socially ostracized for sticking out. As the Japanese saying goes, "The nail that sticks out gets hammered in." A 2006 *New York Times* article noted one *hikikomori* who was bullied at school because his natural talent for baseball put him ahead of his hard-working teammates. The same boy would likely be a hero in the United States!

Michael Zielenziger, who studied the *hikikomori* phenomenon in his book *Shutting Out the Sun,* notes that, while American youth tend to rebel in more aggressive ways, Japanese youth rebel in the Japanese way—by withdrawing. The squeaky wheel doesn't get grease in Japan and, conversely, recluses tend to fade from view in America. But the *hikikomori are* getting attention—if only because they are hiding out in their parents' homes. Psychologists pore over the problem, parents reluctantly seek counseling, and a program called *New Start* sends out "rental sisters" who are trained to befriend and mentor these boys into their program and eventually into society. And just as youthful protestors have been forces of change in our society, the *hikikomori* are slowly shaking up a society where change itself upsets the illusion of perfect harmony.

The contrasts between American extroversion and Japanese introversion reveal the limitations, as Jung put it, of a "one-sided attitude." The ancient *Tai Chi* symbol captures the ways opposites flow into each other: go too far in one direction, and

the need for the other becomes apparent. The *yang* is the bright force associated with extroversion and the West, with Sun and Heaven. *Yang* energy is active and masculine, and flows forward, upward, and outward. The *yin* is the dark force associated with introversion and the East. The energy of *yin* flows backward, downward, and inward, and has characteristics of femininity, stillness, passivity, and the life of the unconscious. Moon and Earth capture the essence of *yin.*

Note that *yin* harbors a nucleus of *yang,* and visa versa. The nucleus is akin to Jung's *shadow* concept—the denied part of us that haunts our dreams until we pay attention. Applied to America and Japan, this may explain both the fear and the fascination between our two cultures: America's hunger for all things Eastern, from yoga to manga, and Japan's obsession with American trends. Of the latter, Reid noted that, when he lived in Japan, it was extremely difficult to find a T-shirt or cap with a Japanese slogan on it: everything was in English. He shared some comical translations, such as "I love you guitar to dying" on one T-shirt, and commented that getting it right was not the point—getting it in English *was.*

Though Zielenziger's book focuses on a problem in Japanese society, the author acknowledges the positive side of Japan's conservatism, as well as the ways Japan and the U.S. have each mastered only part of the equation:

> The gentle, minimalist character of traditional Japan, that which seeks harmony with nature instead of trying to tame it, and finds beauty in the sparse rather than in the abundant, has much to teach a contemporary world now confronted by physical and resource limits...If Japan has yet to acknowledge the crucial role of the individual in creating social responsibility, then we in America have failed to articulate the sense of community and community obligation needed to mitigate the excesses of individualism.

Here is the paradox of introversion in society: Individualism gives each of us a voice, but excesses of individualism result in a cacophony of voices, allowing only the loudest to be heard. So how do we remain individuals and introverts too? Norden and Japan are both free societies with introverted values, but they both have the advantage (and disadvantage) of housing a relatively homogeneous population. Interestingly, MBTI® research in other countries tends to replicate the fifty-fifty split between introverts and extroverts—which, if the split holds for Norden and Japan—means that there may be a lot of frustrated extroverts out there!

The reality is, though, that if America is truly "of the people," we are not as extroverted as we've been led to believe. If we are not ready to pull up our stakes and head north, east, or in another direction that holds promise, perhaps we can import some of these introverted ideas:

- Look to like-minded subgroups to provide you islands of calm, whether you know the people in the group (i.e., introverted friends) or not (i.e., quiet people at the coffeehouse).
- Claim the power of silence and vagueness. American businessmen have been known to put themselves at a disadvantage by too readily putting their cards on the table while their Japanese counterparts stay calmly silent or provide a vague response. The quiet, less aggressive party is able to feel out the talker, gaining the advantage of more information and more time.
- Dare to find wildness in nature—there are fewer people there.
- Create space for yourself by planting a garden, clearing clutter, or honoring a mundane task.
- Physical hardiness and a strong work ethic allow you to thrive in solitary places.
- See the wisdom in holding back, staying put, and seeking harmony.
- Some realities can be seen better in the dark.

INTROVERTIA

Though we can identify societies that nurture introversion, and there are many more to explore, the ideal society, our "Introvertia," is best designed from the inside out. What kind of society would you design? What features would you take from places you've been or places you imagine? To start the brainstorming, here are a few good ideas received from a few good introverts:

- We would redesign our urban model around greenspace. —Doug
- My ideal society is a dark coffee shop with lots of couches. Smoking is allowed, but there is a great air filtration

system. Dark, chill, with lots of corners and nooks and crannies to hide in. Then, if you want to socialize, you could ask someone for a lighter.—Jessica

- Manzanillo, Mexico, was the best place I have ever been. There, everybody dances, but I didn't feel very good about my skills (or lack thereof) and didn't want to. To sum it up, they didn't care at all what decision I made and smiled and had a great time with me anyway.—Solveig

- Anywhere where there are vast expanses of water (lake, rivers, marshlands) or land (mown grass, prairie grass fields), or extensive vistas (Grand Canyon, Washington State waterways). [A] society wherein people spoke slowly, clearly, and sparsely. Sort of like West Texas and Montana (ranching country). Activities rely more on accomplishments and less on social interaction as outcomes.—Phil

- Provide nondenominational "chapels" or gardens, places like the English gardens, designed to accommodate *melancholia*—what used to be an accepted form of social isolation.—Doug

- I loved living in Chicago. People in Chicago don't make eye contact with one another when they walk down the street. I didn't realize how comfortable I was with that until I moved away! And there's something to do ALL of the time in ANY price range.—Lisa

- Portland has it all…including…its own chapter of the now international Church of Craft…where an introvert is free to craft away in a supportive environment and explore the work of others without feeling pressured into mandatory mingling. We even let extroverts join us…we're just that kind of open, gutsy group! —Suzanne

- I like the café village culture of Europe, because there's cultural acceptance for finding a niche in the corner of a café or of the plaza and staying there all day. No one's rushing you out to accommodate the next customer. —Doug

- No one would ever need to speak. We would communicate with thoughts and emotions, leaving only room for the 100 percent truth. If we felt a need to speak or sing, that would be accepted just the same, but we still could not lie. Our emotions would give us away. Also I think it would be nice to have some outward sign of feeling. For example, many animals' ears naturally turn a certain way to show how they feel. Back shows discomfort, to the side shows content, and forward demonstrates attention and awareness.—Solveig
- For me, it would be first and foremost a much quieter and less rude society. Fewer bars, more walking paths. Less idle conversation, more reading. Fewer incursions into other nations' affairs, more resources devoted to domestic problems.—Don
- It would be an island in the Caribbean with a handful of inhabitants from various countries. We would speak different languages, so that our communication would be more basic and nonverbal. The warmth would allow freedom of movement and little need for clothing. Havens of nature would provide privacy and inspiration. A new mode of transportation would allow travel to any point on earth without requiring a large airport.—Laurie
- There's no sweeter feeling than when I'm driving on the back roads of West Virginia and no one knows where I am. There's something delicious about the world not knowing where I am.—Doug

As you scan the places you dreamed of as a child, the havens you've discovered in your travels, and the ideas presented here, notice what themes emerge for you. Write or paint or just imagine your version of *Introvertia*. Then consider how you might create this society within your society. Can you bring in elements of *Introvertia* through your décor or your lifestyle? Even a small symbol can serve as a reminder. When I visited the Amazon, a shaman told me that I had the spirit of a pink dolphin, "quiet and intelligent." As I swam in the same waters that provided a home for these dolphins, I realized that I have always felt at home in water, that I gave my boys "dolphin rides" when they were little, and that I love swimming underwater. I have a carved pink dolphin in my office to remind me of this submerged home.

Imagine importing pieces of the puzzle from the places you love and putting them together in the center of your life. In the next section, *The Introvert's Wish List,* we bring in some of these pieces and discuss how to set them up where you live, love, work, and play. You'll have plenty of room to customize the vision as you go.

Part II:
The Introvert's Wish List

Chapter 6:
A Room of Your Own

A woman must have money and a room of her own if she is to write fiction.

—Virginia Woolf

Ahhh, a room of your own. When you were a kid, you may have been lucky enough to have your own room: a place where you kept *your* stuff, a place where you could be in charge, a place that reflected—whether through your stuffed animals or your rock band posters—what you cared about. Perhaps you even posted a "Keep Out" sign on the door. If you shared a room, you probably had a side or area that was yours. When my sister and I graduated from our bunks in the hallway to a shared room, I established an invisible dividing line between my side and my sister's—it cut right through the middle of the double bed. My side was Japanese-style, neat and uncluttered. My extroverted sister's side was a mess. What I had were drawers, little boxes, a red vinyl pencil case—containers that held my treasures. And I had my journals. I hid things in secret places. Private space was not a given in my home, so I learned to create it everywhere I could.

Think about your room as a child. What items did you keep there? How did you decorate the space? Whether you got to pick the bedspread or not, your style was reflected in how you tended the space—packrat or minimalist, slob or neat freak, even your clutter reflected you. Maybe you established a room out of doors, in a tree house or shed, on the grass under a weeping willow, deep in the city or deep in the woods.

Where is your room today? Perhaps this seems an odd question. Adults don't have a room—we get the whole apartment or house, plus an office or cubicle at work. As kids, we had to keep our stuff in just one room. Sure, it's nice to have influence over more spaces in the world—choosing where we live, decorating, and so on. But being so spread out has a downside: we no longer have a built-in "retreat center," a place where we can be assured of privacy, a place that is not decorated for visitors.

After all that work of getting out of our parents' home, declaring our independence and setting up a life of our own, many of us discover that we have no *place* of our own. One day we look around and notice that we're living in a house with a shared kitchen, a shared living room with the TV blaring, shared bathrooms, and a shared bedroom. Help!

It seems a cruel product of adulthood that we leave behind the concept of "my room"—that place that represents you, and *only* you. Maybe you do have such a place. For many of us it's an office at home. I think computers are popular for introverts, in part, because they give a message of "I'm busy" to potential intruders. Authors, musicians, and artists can often more easily justify designating space for an office or studio. But even if you can afford an extra "me" room—a room with no other function—you are in the minority if you feel free enough to make it truly *yours*.

YOUR DREAM ROOM

If you ask most people to describe their dream house, many of us could describe the dwelling in detail. But because the concept of "my room" fades with adult consciousness, you probably haven't given much thought to your dream *room*. So, here's your chance.

For now, we're looking at indoor space—a place you can go to anytime, even when it's pouring rain outside. We'll start by constructing your dream room on paper. You can do this in the way that best fits you:

- Jot notes in this book—it's yours, after all!
- Jot notes somewhere else—journal, blank sheet, blank wall.
- Draw or paint your vision if you're artistically inclined.

Now go ahead and get what you need. It's okay—I'll mark your place.

As you proceed with this exercise, please do not attempt to be practical or realistic. This is your *dream* room. Another thing: this room does not have to please anyone else, so you don't need to stick to conventional rules of decorating. Think kid's room with the kid in charge. Here are some choices to consider:

This is where you left off while getting your supplies.

Basics:
What size of a room suits you?
What kind of atmosphere or feeling are you going for?

Location:
Is your room attached to your home or freestanding?
Do you want to face the morning sun or the setting sun?
Do you prefer to be on ground level or an upper floor?
What view do you prefer?

Ceiling, Doors and Windows:
How high is your ceiling?
How much glass do you want and where—windows, skylights, walls?
Where is the entry to your room?
Do you want a separate door going outside?
Would you like your own deck, balcony, or patio?

Interior Elements:

Would you like carpet, hardwood, or tile?
Do you want heavy drapes, blinds, or no window coverings?
Would you like a fireplace? What type?
Do you prefer bright or subdued lighting?
Do you want a closet or highly organized storage area?

Let's pause here. Before we put any items in your room, imagine arriving here after a day out in public—a day of interruptions, noise, and talk. You have longed to retreat to this room all day. What are your needs? How do you want to re-energize?

As you consider the room's function, what do you want in this room with you? Maybe you don't want anything—you just want to sit or lie down on the floor and breathe in the space. If you'd like to add more, here are some random ideas to stimulate your thinking:

Style Options:

❑ Pillows, cushions, and soft throws
❑ Clean lines
❑ Antiques, Persian rugs
❑ High-tech, futuristic
❑ Color
❑ Earthy, adobe
❑ TV or movie theme

Bring It In or Leave It Out?

❑ Tall bookcases with ladders to reach the higher shelves
❑ One really good book
❑ Great sound system and a library of CDs
❑ Desk—antique or modern
❑ Easel and paints
❑ Computer
❑ Guitar or grand piano
❑ Journal, notepads, pens, and stationery
❑ Couch or daybed
❑ Huge soft chair and ottoman

❏ One wall serves as a movie screen
❏ Television
❏ High-tech equipment
❏ Art—paintings, sculpture, pottery
❏ Animal companion(s)

Let's take things a bit further: Are there any super-gaudy items you want to include that others would disapprove of? These may include toys, souvenirs, or just stuff you like but don't allow yourself. Think of your quirkiest desires, and go for it! It's your room, and you can offend if you want to.

<u>Only in *Your* **Room:**</u>
❏ Leg lamp
❏ Pink flamingo lawn ornaments
❏ Strings of lights
❏ Favorite action hero collection
❏ Barbie collection
❏ Neon
❏ Train and miniature village
❏ Duck decoys
❏ Velvet Elvis painting
❏ Rock collection

At this point, you may find your room getting too cluttered. Feel free to remove items or expand the room, or both. Ask yourself which five items you would keep in the room if everything else had to go. This will give you clarity on what you value. Take a moment to move out anything that gets in the way of the free

> ## SPECIFICATIONS FOR DON'S ROOM:
> - Big screen TV
> - Excellent sound system
> - Vast music collection
> - Kick-ass computer
> - Serious exercise equipment
> - Good books
> - Comfortable furniture
> - Day bed
> - Beautiful views
> - Musical instruments
> - Sports memorabilia
> - Mellow cat and/or dog

expression of who you are. Bring in anything required for that expression.

Rest. Look around. Know that you can change your dream room anytime you like, and you can even create different models and pick your favorite.

FROM DREAM TO REAL

I had you do this exercise to begin to break you of the habit of decorating for *other* people and to begin making space for your inner life. Do you find yourself getting things ready—cleaning, fluffing pillows, arranging fresh flowers—only when you have company coming? Or if you do make things "just right" for you, do you relax and enjoy the space? It seems ironic that so many American homes maintain formal living rooms that are for display only, not for living! And, for introverts, the family room may easily become overstimulating—that is, if you have a family. From a young age, I was aware that the center of the home, the living room (we didn't have a formal one), was not my space—and it's still not. I fought this reality for years, but now happily relinquish the space much of the time to my husband and boys. I go to my room.

If you do not have a room that is yours alone, it's time to create such a space. You may have an office that you use more than other family members—this may work. Or perhaps you have a room that is just being used for storage. If you're only using a room a couple times a year—i.e., guest room or dining room—consider taking it over. Depending on your climate, a screened-in porch or conservatory may work. Of course, you'll want to talk with other family members about what you're doing, but do so only after you're convinced that this is a great idea. Believe me, it is.

A room of your own provides "the still point of the turning world," to use T. S. Eliot's imagery. It's a place, like the kid's room, that you know is there for you. It's a place for the items that have meaning only to you. As you look around at your things, your priorities, you become more of who you are. Your room becomes your mirror.

Even if your space is too limited right now, mapping out your room on paper will set the course toward that reality. Years ago, I created a "Discovery Journal," a bound artist's book that I filled with collages, an idea provided by Sarah Breathnach in her wonderful book, *Simple Abundance*. The idea is to cut out images you are drawn to (even if you don't know *why* you are drawn to them), arrange them on a blank page, and glue them down. I found myself collecting pictures of rooms, interior décor and, repeatedly, colored tile. A series of events had us moving across country and in a position to build a house of our own design. I pulled out my Discovery Journal, and my house was in there! I even brought the journal to a tile supplier and used it as a design guide. My dream became a reality.

Years later, when we moved to our current, older home, I claimed the small den with large windows and a built-in bookcase. I was excited that there was a closet in the room with built-in drawers. The plaster on the walls was cracked in places, which provided me a great opportunity: I started a collage! At the time of this writing, I have half a wall completely covered in images of what I love. My mirror.

So, whatever it is you dream up, as Goethe said, "begin it."

> ## SPECIFICATIONS FOR INGRID'S ROOM:
>
> I'd like my room to be most of all quiet. Ideally a screened-in porch on a nice day is perfect (again, as long as it's quiet). I'd like a comfortable sofa to sit/lie on and lots of reading material (preferably a combination of magazines, books, and newspapers), plus a pencil and eraser and semi-complicated crossword puzzles. Finally, I'd like a quiet companion, however, only the nonspeaking kind. My dog would fulfill that role.

ROOM OUTSIDE

For many introverts, there is no better shelter than the one provided by nature: the endless sky above; the trees, mountains or infinite horizon all around; the good, solid earth under foot. Finding a private space outside is harder for some of us than for others. Some of us have a semi-private backyard, others have vast woods out back, and still others have only small or shared patches of green in the midst of concrete.

A neighbor of mine recently called me over to show me a "room" she had built along the shady side of her cottage-sized house. As I entered the space, I felt the boundaries of her room, even though there were no walls enclosing it. She had used tree stump slabs and tiny white rocks to construct a path leading in; an arbor set between a tree and the house to form the doorway; a bench, easel, and small table made up the furniture; and candles on the ground provided mood lighting. Her paints, notebook, and pen were waiting for her on the bench.

The beauty of an outdoor room is that it offers both privacy and expansiveness—the trees around and the sky above. Creating and caring for a private outdoor space can provide a Zen-like sense of calm. When I was little, my sister and I created a playhouse in the woods by raking little clearings between the trees and designating them as rooms. We made hallways between the rooms, and even planted a little garden outside. For furnishings, we scavenged the junk pile nearby, which provided an endless supply of treasures. As I looked back, there was something in the raking itself—in the founding of my own space in nature—that gave me immense pleasure. I think of Thoreau and the joy he found in setting up his house in the natural habitat of Walden Pond.

There is a vast difference between the quiet pleasure of tending a private space and the pressure of outdoor work that only improves the view for our neighbors. Both are valid, and an attractive yard is indeed a gift to the neighborhood, but I feel a certain sadness when I pass by a manicured lawn that I know will not enjoy the dance of bare feet. Like the good china, it is not to be touched.

What defines an outdoor room may be very simple: a bistro table and chair where you sit with your coffee and read, a fire pit in the backyard that allows you warmth at night, a rooftop in the city that renders people and cars smaller and the sky bigger. And nature provides many dwelling places—from the natural rock furniture on top of a hill to the walls of tall grass that encircle you when you lay in a meadow.

Just as Jung discovered treasures deep in the unconscious, Emerson found "wild delight" as he lingered in nature. As many solitary explorers have discovered, nature seems to hear and understand, to provide an empathy beyond the capacity of humans. Emerson captures this empathic response in his writings:

SPECIFICATIONS FOR BETH'S ROOM:

- Surrounded by nature, not walls
- A rock overlooking an expanse of mountains that fall into the ocean
- Ancient, wise conifer trees forming a half circle around me
- The smell of the sea and pine needles
- The sound of a stream winding down the slope into the ocean and birds singing, calling to one another
- The feel of the earth beneath me
- Sandy soil that I can run through my fingers
- The knowledge that life surrounds me—life that began before me and will continue after I am gone

If a man would be alone, let him look at the stars...The stars awaken a certain reverence, because though always present, they are inaccessible; but all natural objects make a kindred impression, when the mind is open to their influence...The greatest delight, which the fields and woods minister, is the suggestion of an occult relation between man and the vegetable. I am not alone and unacknowledged. They nod to me, and I to them. The waving of the boughs in the storm, is new to me and old...Nature always wears the colors of the spirit.

OFFICE SPACE

"Office space" is somewhat of an oxymoron these days. *Office Space* (1999) is also a hilarious movie. The following lines between the characters played by Jennifer Aniston and Ron Livingston reflect the contempt employees feel for the cubicle culture of today's office:

Peter: I uh, I don't like my job, and, uh, I don't think I'm gonna go anymore.

Joanna: You're just not gonna go?

Peter: Yeah.

Joanna: Won't you get fired?

Peter: I don't know, but I really don't like it, and, uh, I'm not gonna go.

I would imagine most introverts have fantasized about doing what Peter did—and some have pulled it off. But dropping out is not a viable option for most of us, and many of us spend at least part of our time at an office—*without* an office. The office of today has banished private space in favor of freestanding modules cluttering massive rooms: the dreaded *cubicle.*

In an article for *Fortune* (March 22, 2006), Julie Schlosser reviewed how cubicles were faring thirty years after Robert Propst released his prototype for the enclosure. The article, "Cubicles: The great mistake," noted that Propst, like inventors of tools used in warfare, despised the office culture that grew out of his contribution. Schlosser compared the cubicle to crabgrass that persists in growing despite its lack of popularity:

> Reviled by workers, demonized by designers, disowned by its very creator, it still claims the largest share of office furniture sales—$3 billion or so a year—and has outlived every "office of the future" meant to replace it. It is the Fidel Castro of office furniture.

Office-less office employees, retail personnel, nurses, and administrative staff—to mention only a few—spend a great deal of their day within easy reach of others. Even those of us who have the luxury of a door often feel pressure to keep it open.

What kind of room do you have at work? Mentally go to that place, sit or stand wherever you sit or stand, and look around. What is your view? What feelings do you have as you look around? How well can you *think* in this space?

Now exit reality and imagine your ideal workspace. Don't think about your real job or even your profession for the moment. Just think about the kind of space you would love to work in—*your* workspace. As we did for your room, consider size, the view, the lighting, and what you want inside. I'll put in another bookmark so you can go off and do your thinking. You may want to jump back to the first bookmark and use the questions there to get you going.

If you are resisting this exercise, protesting that you have no choice about your work setting, I'll say what I say to my clients: "You have a choice about whether to *like it*." And introverts, in particular, have been told for too long to like it—from the team meetings to the happy hour after work. I'm not suggesting we start whining and feeling depressed about our work setting; we may already be doing both. What I am suggesting is that we do what we do best: seek inner clarity. As you compare your ideal and real work settings, you will start to get that clarity.

This is where you left off while getting your supplies.

Whining is an indication of powerlessness, as when the child whines about going to school. Inner clarity is a source of power: the clearer you are about what you want, the more prepared you are to act when the time is ripe. And the time may be ripe now.

James Meyer, who specializes in placing IT (Information Technology) professionals, saw the loss of identity that came with the cubicle culture, and has helped to usher in an increasingly popular option: telecommuting—commuting to work via computer. Working at home has become a standard part of the contracts Meyer negotiates for these highly skilled professionals. "They're much happier," says Meyer, who also works at home, "only now they complain about coming in for a staff meeting."

But IT specialists aren't the only employees working from home, also referred to as *teleworking*. Here's an idea that environmentalists and conservative policymakers can agree on. In addition to saving energy and reducing pollution, spreading out work is being promoted as a solution to terrorism—take that Osama! A 2007 survey by CDW Corporation reported that forty-four percent of Federal employees now have the option to telework. And, as Meyer observed, telecommuters are happier employees. Results of a 2006 survey by *Money* magazine and Salary.com, reported by Rob Kelley for CNNMoney.com, revealed that satisfied workers had the most work-from-home options and "the most stressed workers were also least able to telecommute, with only a third saying it was an option for them at work." The report also found that flexibility in hours and ease of getting time off made for happier employees. And these happier employees weren't slackers: the most satisfied employees actually worked eleven hours more per week than the least satisfied group!

> The brain is a wonderful organ. It starts working the moment you get up in the morning and does not stop until you get into the office.
>
> —Robert Frost

Schlosser's piece in *Fortune* also discussed the telecommuting trend, as well as the office located in a "third space"—usually a quiet coffeehouse. The home office and third space alternatives were envisioned by the sixties' revolutionary Stewart Brand, author of *The Whole Earth Catalog*, who has worked out of a converted shipping container as well as a beached fishing boat.

Even if the time is *not* ripe for you to claim your own office space, here are some ways you can bring a sense of "mine" to the space you have:

- *Take your breaks!* When the clock says it's time for your break or for lunch, get out. Start a list of places you can go to reenergize. A client of mine lamented giving up smoking because she missed the "smoke breaks." Think of introvert time-outs as *breathing* breaks. If your break isn't long enough to allow a complete retreat, have a book or journal handy—both send the message, "I want to be alone."

- *Work unconventional hours.* If you can flex, try working earlier or later than your colleagues. Working a weekend day in exchange for a workday can be a refreshing switch: an empty office on the weekend, and a quieter world on a weekday.
- *Claim the space you have.* Bring in an item from your room at home, something quirky that only you could think of. Clear clutter. Every so often, close your eyes and breathe. Let your body language communicate, "I'm working."
- *Find alternative space AT the office.* Retreat to a spare conference room to work on a project. Volunteer to make a run to the post office, library, or storage facility and savor the time in your car. In the sitcom *Scrubs,* medical interns used the supply closet as a hideout when they needed to have a panic attack or a good cry. If you seek private space, you are much more likely to find it.

Regardless of where you roam in the course of your day, don't forget to take your mind with you—the ultimate private space. Practice being honest with yourself. Make note of what you like and don't like, what feels right and what feels wrong. Give mental space to your desires. Seek clarity. Make revisions as needed. And be very, very kind to yourself. Your space will expand. I promise.

Chapter 7:
The Time to Think

Men fear thought as they fear nothing else on earth, more than ruin, more even than death. Thought is subversive and revolutionary, destructive and terrible; thought is merciless to privilege, established institutions, and comfortable habit. Thought looks into the pit of hell and is not afraid.
—Bertrand Russell

You have your day scheduled out, given over to the expectations of others. You brace yourself for what's ahead. Then you get a call. The day is cancelled; everyone who needed you is down with a three-day virus.

Is there anything more delicious? You know what I'm talking about. We don't like others to be sick, but we *love* others to cancel. We become giddy at the prospect of "found" time—time without plans or expectations. Time to think. Time between time.

Why is it so hard to plan this kind of time? We take a day off and then feel guilty that we're not getting enough done or not having enough *fun* — or both. Found time is a gift; planned time becomes a demand, which, paradoxically, is not time at all. I return again to Whitman's *Song of the Open Road* and imagine him looking in every direction and inhaling "great draughts of space." What if we could not only experience such space but also inhale great draughts of *time*?

For an introvert, ample time would provide a cushion around activity—the mental space we need to reflect, to make meaning, to find inspiration. There would be lots of "time between time," and introverts would thrive.

This option is not just available in fantasy or in the introvert's version of heaven. Just as we can reclaim our space, we can indulge in time. First, let's look at what we're up against.

TIME POVERTY

In America, time has become a commodity, and a scarce one at that. We invent more and more ways of saving time, only to find even more ways to spend it. When we say that "time is money," we make time a product—and produce, we must! When we say that "time is money," we really mean that money is *more important* than time: that time has value to the extent that it is redeemable in money. The introvert mode of thinking *first* is not valued, because the thinking time is not a tangible product. Even if the thinking time is *on its way* to being a tangible product, we believe time is scarce, so we can't afford much of that kind of time. Those who think on their feet, or simply *use* their feet and their mouths, seem to be making good on the time-money trade. In our American "just do it" society, *doing* takes the lead over *knowing*. Value is associated with what you produce, what you show to the world. And, like cheap talk, credit cards allow us to show much, much more—whether or not we have anything real to back it.

Likewise, our technology allows us to do much, much more—whether or not we have the knowledge to back it. But just as the credit card sucks away the borrower's cash and freedom, excessive doing leaves the mind vacant, clueless, and increasingly dependent on, well, "doing." We sit down to think, we become anxious, we pop up again and get busy to restore the *feeling* that we're going somewhere. We have no idea where, but at least we're going there.

> To achieve, you need thought. You have to know what you are doing and that's real power.
>
> —Ayn Rand

THE TICKING BOMB MODEL

Introverts have a hard time keeping up, and this may be our salvation—and *society's* salvation. Introverts shut down when there's too much stimulation. We don't have much choice. A red light flashes, "OVERLOAD," and we know it's time to pull back and think. The only problem is, we don't have *time*. Or at least that's what we're told.

We have built an entire mythology around the idea that there is no time, using phrases like "running out of time" without thought. Do we really run out of time? Or do we run time *out*? And who thought of the term "deadline"? Are we really supposed to be motivated by fear, by the idea that there is not enough, by poverty? When I published my first book and we were doing my final revisions, I was floored when the editor nonchalantly informed me of the *"drop dead* date"—the date when everything, absolutely, had to be in. This was a real industry term! But the associations between unproductive time and death don't stop there. Stop to reflect, and you are "killing time." Such violent language is enough to make anyone anxious!

In our culture, time is chopped up into portions. Time starts and stops, and all along the time bomb ticks. We feel immense guilt if we don't produce in the allotted time chunk. Work starts when the clock says it's time, and it is imperative that you start, too. In our society, time is rigid, stingy, and running out.

It is useful to make agreements about time, and I'll be the first to admit that having a "deadline" helps—but then again, it's the only system I know. But do we really need to be threatened? Have we lost all trust in the creative process?

FROM DEADLINE TO BIRTH TIME

What if we called the target date the "*birth time*" instead? Birthing happens when the project—the baby—is *ready*. Most of the work happens inside, naturally. The pressure builds until that little life *has to* come out. But, as opposed to a *deadline*, the pressure is *internal*. A terrified woman in the throes of labor may want to call the whole thing off, but the creative process takes over, and she is soon looking into the eyes of a completely new human being.

Introverts have direct access to this internal power—the power to birth fully formed ideas, insights, and solutions. People ask me how I'm able to come up with enough material to fill a book. I tell them, "I've been writing this all of my life." An introvert who sits back in a meeting, taking in the arguments, dreamily reflecting on the big picture, may be seen as not contributing—that is, until he works out the solution that all the contributors missed.

The birthing model not only allows time to think, but it allows time to stay alive. We can't really kill time, and we can't really chop time up. We just don't have that much control. Time is time. It will be there whether we run ourselves ragged or sit on the dock of the bay. And, for introverts especially, this is very good news.

For almost twenty years, I have devoted my psychology practice to "rehabilitating desire": helping clients revive desires that have been assaulted by external demands, and restoring their trust in their own desire-based motivation. Though we often think of desire in sexual terms—and sexual desire is a good example of this motivating energy—I use the term in its broader and richer sense. Desire is the seed of intrinsic motivation, the natural impulse to create, to expand, to grow.

People often argue that desire is inherently bad or burdensome, fostering either harmful behavior or greedy consumption. Harmful outcomes do sometimes occur, but they happen when desire is not given the proper attention—and time. A person bent on getting drunk probably does not want to consume toxins and eventually become sick and depressed; she desires a change in her state of mind. She didn't overindulge at all; she *underindulged.* She did not give her desire enough time, thought, or attention. In fact, addictive behaviors usually have more to do with a need to *extinguish* desire. The thinking is: "If I binge, I won't ever be hungry again," or "If I build a huge house with everything I need, I will never have to move." Why in the world would we want to eliminate our experience of hunger or stop exploring new horizons? Because time is running out, of course. We need to figure out how to make babies quicker!

The paradox is, when we use the desire model instead of the death model, everything is easier. Desire, when it is properly nourished, works like pregnancy and birth: once it gets going, there's no stopping it. But birthing

> There is more to life than increasing its speed.
>
> —Gandhi

requires the capacity to hold, to tolerate the growing pressure of what's inside and to patiently wait until it's ready. *This holding capacity is the hallmark of introversion.* And it's extremely powerful. Here's how it works:

- *Step 1: Capture your wishful thinking.* Pay attention to the times you say to yourself, "I wish I could _____," or "Wouldn't it be nice if _____." Sometimes the wish will be for something extravagant; other times you will feel the desire to solve a problem or master something you're working on. You may just want a break. Whatever it is, take note of it. Feelings of desire come up multiple times a day, but we often cover them over before we recognize them. You may want to keep a Desire Notebook. Putting your wishes in writing makes them visible and tangible, and helps you notice emerging themes. **Warning:** *Be prepared for thoughts that interrupt your desiring. They may tell you that what you want is too much to expect, or mockingly ask you, "Who do you think* *you are?" Don't let these thoughts trap you. Just return your attention to the desire.*

- *Step 2: Look into the desire.* When you catch a desire, stay with it. If the desire seems harmful, ask yourself what you're really going for. Cheating on your partner will hurt people (which undermines the desire), but the desire to cheat is telling you something. If you want passion, why should you settle for a part-time solution that leaves you feeling guilty? Think bigger. Sometimes we focus our desires on an *obstacle* to what we want. For example, you may say, "I want this project done," when you *mean* "I hate this project and want it out of my life forever." Or maybe you just want the rest you will earn after completing the project.

- *Step 3: Fantasize.* Once you get to the heart of your desire, give it some room. Think the desire. Visualize the desire. Edit the picture to make it just how you want it. For example, if you want a vacation, imagine where you are, whom you are with (if anyone), what you are doing, and how you are feeling. As your fantasy becomes more specific, your desire will build and gain power.

- *Step 4: Allow new and conflicting desires.* Once you hear the voice of your own desires, you may feel a bit over-whelmed by all that emerges. And sometimes two desires collide—like the desire to play all day and the desire to make money. Holding so much potential can feel over-whelming at times. But this feeling usually comes from the thought that you need to immediately do something with the desire. Though introverts are less prone to this impatience, society's cry to "do" is persistent. Replace the order to *do* with permission to *allow*. Simply allow the new desire, knowing its time may be sooner or later. Let conflicting desires sit side by side.

- *Step 5: Allow fulfillment.* Once you empower the desire within you, it will automatically move toward fulfill-ment. When you feed conflicting desires, you engage your creative capacity to create higher-level solutions.

The more you trust your desires and allow them to emerge, the less effort you have to expend. You notice an ad in the paper, a friend calls with a proposal, you are moved by an invisible force to act. All that is left for you to do is to respond and say "thank you."

NATURE'S RHYTHM, SOCIETY'S RHYTHM

In his fascinating book, *Time Shifting,* Stephan Rechtschaffen discusses another factor in how we experience time: *entrainment.* Entrainment is what happens when you set two pendulum clocks to swing at different rates, and then put them side-by-side. They start to move together. Since this phenomenon was discovered in the 17th century, applications have been found everywhere, from synchronized menstrual cycles among women who live together, to separate heart muscle cells that pulse together after being placed together. In the same way, entrainment affects our sense of time. People speed up in the hubbub of an airport, whether or not they need to. You tap your foot to the beat of the music. A mother holds a sleeping baby over her chest, and the two begin to breathe in perfect harmony.

When we were more dependent on nature and its seasonal fluctuations, the rhythms of time were cyclical. Now we experience time as a straight line with a beginning and an end—or many disconnected beginnings and endings. Rechtschaffen discusses the overall shift in our rhythm that came with the Industrial Revolution:

> If the days, the seasons, even lifetimes come around again, then time never runs out. What is not completed in the circle of today may be accomplished tomorrow. If not this year, then the next; if not in this lifetime, then in another...By contrast, our modern rhythm is distinctly *unnatural,* mirroring society's pull, not the magnetism of the earth. We're taught to think quickly,

act quickly, accomplish quickly…We have superimposed on nature the rhythms of greed, of materialism, of "having it all."

Rechtschaffen also reminds us that nature is still with us and many different rhythms are available in modern life.

THE RHYTHM OF INTROVERSION

For better and for worse, introverts are more naturally attuned to nature's rhythms. Because we are internally oriented, we can more easily entrain with the rhythms of the body; and the rhythms of the body respond to the cycles of nature—i.e., light and dark, heat and cold.

As we discussed in Chapter 1, introverts have been found to experience a higher level of mental arousal on an ongoing basis. We seek to reduce the added stimulation offered by society. By contrast, extroverts, who experience a lower level of arousal, look to society for excitement. It follows that extroverts would be more easily entrained with the rhythms of society, and another set of studies support this contention.

These studies, reported in *The Journal of Personality and Social Psychology* between the years 2000 and 2006 (one included over six thousand subjects from thirty-nine different countries) consistently found that extroverts, when compared to introverts, are more responsive to external rewards, especially those of a social nature. Extroverts also seemed to be better at controlling and maintaining consistent and pleasant moods. Introverts, on the other hand, experienced greater variability in their mood states, fluctuations that were less dependent on external rewards.

The findings suggested that extroverts have an advantage, but I read the results a different way. If the goal is to be consistently pleasant, extroverts do seem to have the advantage. But if the goal is to be attuned to the life cycle and its creative potential, I think introverts have the edge. We only need to reconnect with our power source.

When I first saw these findings on extroverts and pleasant-ness, I was pissed (again), and I figured out *why*. I have been bothered for a while now by a New Age trend that, at its extreme, suggests that thought control can and should elimi-nate negative feelings. This, to echo Rechtschaffen, is *unnatural*—it is flow without the ebb, day without night, expression without examination, yang without yin. And this societal orientation excludes introverts.

But, as quickly as I identified my anger, I realized that I don't really care—demonstrating both my fluctuating mood and my lack of response to social rewards. The extroverts can have society. I have nature.

To come full circle, as introverts like to do, *time to think* is not only a luxury for introverts; it is a *necessity*. We need to pull our pendulums away from social rhythms and access the life-giving power of our own minds—our wonderfully aroused minds. Let's look at some ways to expand time.

Shift from "take" to "give." I've been holding onto an article for years, waiting for the time I had need of it. It's a piece I found in *Parabola* magazine, titled "Learning to Die," by Brother David Steindl-Rast. In the article, the Benedictine monk discusses the awareness that comes with the "rule of St. Benedict," which is to "have death at all times before one's eyes." The death he talks about is not the artificial death imposed by goals, but quite the opposite: the *giving over* of goals, purpose, control. Throughout his article, he reveals how the language of "taking" is embedded into our thinking, and how this mentality has created "an 'underdeveloped nation' with regard to meaningful living." He observes: "We say we take time; but we really live only if we *give* time to what *takes* time. If you take a seat, it is not a very comfortable way of sitting down but if you let the seat take you that's more like it." To Steindl-Rast, this giving over, this attitude of "leisure" is a *virtue*.

Practice giving. *Give* time to what you value. *Give up* a little control. Work and play from a position of abundance, from an attitude of leisure.

Bring your pendulum with you. Remember that half of us are introverted, so we have a huge impact on entrainment. Regularly calibrate your pendulum to your breath, to the rhythm of nature, to the pace of your thoughts. When you are among people, you'll feel more pulls to adjust your pendulum. Instead of focusing on the loudest and fastest, though, look at the quiet introvert reading in the corner, the grass below you, or consider how long it took to construct the building you are in. In conversations, ground yourself—gravity opposes entrainment—and draw on the following Bill of Rights for support:

- Unless someone is bleeding or choking or otherwise at risk of imminent demise, you have a right to think about it.
- Someone else's pressure is *their* pressure. You have a right to let them keep it.
- If someone makes a request and demands an immediate response, say "no." It is easier to change a "no" to a "yes" than it is to get out of something.
- You have a right to not know until you know, especially when you're asked a big question. We all carry around a sense of knowing—that internal, inexplicable sense of when something is or isn't right, but we can't access that sense while under pressure.
- You have a right to obtain more information. If you don't know, find out more.
- You do not have to jump in with affirming comments when you don't feel it. You have a right to remain silent.

Flow in circular time. This principle has been an immense help to me in writing this book. With my deadlines, both internal and external, I can get caught up in linear time, trying to push forward from beginning to end. If I'm stuck, I keep pushing. I try to flow without ebbing. I resist nature.

The introverted, or *yin*, principle teaches us to go back, to reflect. When we marry this concept with the forward-moving *yang,* we start to cooperate with nature and ride its energy. So now, when I'm stuck, I just flow around the block and return to it later. The cycling back works so well that I often fill in the blanks soon after I move forward. It's that old phenomenon of losing something: when you finally give up the search, you instantly remember where you last placed it.

In my moving-forward mode, I was also accumulating piles of material to read and organize. I kept telling myself that I couldn't afford to attend to the piles, even though I was eager to dig in to the material. Something hit me as I was writing about Japan and its *yin* nature. I gave—here's where I would normally say "spent" or "used" or "took"—a day to the piles. I gave a precious writing day to reading, creating files for material on each chapter, clearing the space in my office. I decided to call it my *yin day,* and to have a yin day every week. Now my papers don't turn into piles. In Judeo-Christian traditions, the Sabbath is a kind of yin day, a day to rest from labor, to reflect, to atone for sins, and to express gratitude for blessings. College students know the joy of a yin day after finals, when they get to scoop up all the scattered papers and attend to the wonderfully mundane needs that they neglected while studying for finals.

When we embrace the option to cycle back, we not only get a chance to attend to neglected details, we can also reevaluate and correct the mindless agreements we make while socially entrained. For example, if you say "yes" to an engagement because you can't think of an excuse, you can go back and correct the conversation.

Read or watch time-benders. Shake up your sense of time by entering a new dimension. Pick up a DVD of old *Twilight Zone* episodes. Read *Einstein's Dreams* by Alan Lightman. In his brilliant, beguiling, and extremely short novel, each of the genius' dreams create a different world operating on a different time system: in one, time flows backwards; in another, people live forever; and in another, people live their lives in one day.

Embrace limbo. If you have had the experience of traveling to another country, you know that getting there can try your patience. I think back to the experience of cruising the

Caribbean with my husband and how much we had to go through to just get to the boat—airplane, bus transport, customs, all with maze-like corrals for waiting in line. Waiting, waiting, waiting. I remember thinking of all the time we were wasting in these uncomfortable settings. Then the thought occurred to me, "If we have this much time to waste, we have time." What I realized is that the process of getting there was transforming my sense of time. After a period of huffing and checking my watch, I had to submit to a different pace. Once I did this, I was really on vacation.

It can feel wonderful to indulge in time, to wander aimlessly, to sit blankly. I especially enjoy sitting with the warm sun on my face, knowing I could move, but deciding that would be too much trouble. Just letting time pass, just breathing the air. Letting time pass. How wonderful.

"Time is short, but it is wide."
"How beautiful it is to do nothing and then rest afterwards."

—Spanish sayings

You don't need to be on vacation to have this experience. Just decide to let time pass. Allow yourself to shift from feeling you have to race time to feeling you have time, all the time in the world. And you will.

Chapter 8:
The Right to
Retreat

It's cluttered. It's cramped. It's noisy. Buzzing, chattering, piles fill this world.

I was raised in this place. I had a hard time following the rules. I got tired of buzzing.

One day, when I was carrying my daily load of clutter, I heard a voice from beyond. Now with piles so high, I'd never heard the beyond. But Beyond called, "I am sky. I am wide." I said, "Shh, you can't say wide. You'll get arrested." Sky replied, "I can't be held." I said, "Can you hold me?" Sky replied, "I have plenty of room," and her gusting winds took me up and away.

I landed in a meadow. I heard, for the first time— nothing. I danced and did somersaults, lay down in a bed of grass, felt the breeze.

And for the first time, I heard my heart, and I knew who I was.

—Laurie Helgoe

In the longer version of this monologue, *Clutteria*, I describe a cartoon world committed to constant buzzing. The laws of Clutteria prohibit listening, televisions are on at all times, and conversation competitions are held regularly. All citizens must contribute to the clutter piles, which shut out any awareness of worlds beyond. Citations are written for anyone attempting to organize the piles. And escaping is extremely difficult.

Escaping is also extremely pleasurable. I was well into my thirties, and well into my therapy, before I allowed myself to indulge a long-held fantasy of taking a retreat—all by myself. To a married and working mother of two small boys, my increasingly frequent and subversive fantasy of leaving everything troubled me. These were people I *loved*, people who *needed me*. So when I realized that I could leave everyone and still *have* them, I was giddy.

I carefully researched the setting for my retreat, calling a number of B&Bs within driving distance but *beyond* my familiar turf. I located one in the woods of Wisconsin, near the tiny artist village of Stockholm. The B&B owners made a policy of keeping themselves scarce, except for the brief time when they serve your made-to-order breakfast at the time you specify and in the location you specify. This was my place!

My experience there was magical. I went through the requisite dip in mood initially, feeling the emptiness of leaving Clutteria. I settled into my small suite with its spring-cleaned freshness: four-poster bed, white linens, windows looking out to the tiny road and surrounding woods, and big, generous towels and candles waiting by a whirlpool tub. I was happy to have a little desk for my books and journal. The house was quiet, so I could freely snoop in the sitting room and kitchen.

What to do? I could go into town—I did need something to eat. I could sprawl out on the bed and read or write. I could go for a walk outside. I felt a brief panic, a reverberation of my entrainment to pressured rhythms: "*Decide*. Make the *right* choice. You've been waiting for this—it had better be good."

The panic washed over. I entered boredom. I slowly started to hear the silence and feel the space. I became a captive audience to my quiet inner voice—that soothing NPR voice that gently notes the profound simplicities of life. I wrote. I lounged. I went into town and savored dinner and dessert alone. I sat by the fire pit that night, tended by the resident singer-songwriter and housekeeper. I saw stars like I had never seen, and ever so often, one would drop from the sky. I had a quiet conversation with the young woman, with much space in between. The next day, I walked a trail through the woods to a place they called "the point"—a huge rock jutting out over a vast glen, a pristine lake in the distance. This room with a view was mine, and I settled there, shedding my backpack and shirt, pulling out my journal and pen, and reclining on the warm rock in the sun.

After lingering there for a timeless time, I packed up and started walking back. As I reentered the woods, I spontaneously broke into a run, feeling a lightness and energy I had never experienced. I bounded into a broad meadow and gleefully reclined in the cool, tall grass, creating another room. I thought of my mother, who had died two years before. I remembered her hanging clothes on the line, and the wonderful feeling of a damp sheet kissing my cheek. A poem spilled out of me into my journal. During my next trip into town, I found a lovely handmade book for my poems. I told the woman helping me about my memory and, upon her request, I read the poem to her. Tears streamed down my face. I hadn't grieved this until now.

WHAT IS A RETREAT?

As the term implies, a retreat is a backing away, a withdrawal, an experience in the realm of *yin*, an act of introversion. A retreat can be a ten-minute break or an extended escape—such as Paul Gauguin's two-year artistic sabbatical in Tahiti—but we usually think of a retreat as a weekend or vacation-length trip "away from it all." For an introvert, retreating is the ultimate indulgence: an inner life binge that fills our depleted energy stores. Retreats, whether contemplative or adventure-oriented, provide a sanctioned and temporary way for us to step away from our worldly pursuits. This stepping away provides a perspective that we cannot obtain while in the midst of things. This is particularly important when we live in an extroverted culture that, like Clutteria, pressures us to keep buzzing and to stay unconscious. Retreats can also help us draw from a greater source of sustenance, whether we see that source as nature, a higher power or the inner self, or all of the above.

How Do I Know When to Go?

Going through the Motions. When you feel like you're living on automatic pilot, when pleasures diminish and life feels dull, it's time to retreat.

"Too Many Notes." If you've seen the movie *Amadeus,* you probably recall the scene in which the king complains about the complexity of Mozart's new composition: "Too many notes." Now this phrase comes to me whenever I feel overstimulated. When the clutter of life has confused your priorities, when you don't know what you're doing here, when it's too noisy to hear your thoughts, it's time to retreat.

Decision Time. When you're about to make an important decision in your life, and you're having a hard time knowing your own mind, it's time to retreat.

Worn out. When you find yourself tired, susceptible to illness, you can't sleep or can't wake up, when your energy is depleted, it's time to retreat.

Burned out. When the creativity is lacking, apathy sets in, and you feel you have little to give, it's time to retreat.

Just wanting to go. If you retreat in response to desire rather than deprivation, the deprivation may never come.

It's the season for your retreat. Recurring retreats become a touchstone for renewal. When the time comes, you are ready to retreat, and the retreat is ready for you.

A SOCIETY IN SEARCH OF INTROVERSION

Perhaps our society's need for introversion is best reflected in the explosion of retreat centers across the United States. The website www.findthedivine.com lists over 1,700 retreat location in the U.S. and Canada, and www.retreatsonline.com provides a listing of over two thousand retreats worldwide. The tricky thing is, as retreats become a commercialized cultural phenomenon, they run the risk of losing their "away" quality. Many retreats are marketed as high-end luxuries providing spas, classes, health-related programs, and special diets. Getting a little pampering may be just the thing: who wouldn't welcome a massage and well-prepared food? But some of these programs have a decidedly extroverted feel, and others transform retreating into another goal-oriented investment—lose weight, get healthy! I am reminded of an episode of *Sex in the City* in which the girlfriends gossip all the way through their yoga session, even as they hold their poses. Beware of extroverts in retreat center clothing!

We even dare to use the word "retreat" for mandatory, task-oriented work meetings held in an alternative setting. The one time I sacrificed a weekend for such a retreat was enough—I felt trapped and restricted in the enclosed circle of work associates. Another television image comes to mind: Michael Scott, the overly zealous boss of *The Office*, corralling his staff into one painful bonding experience after another.

> Violent passions are formed in solitude. In the busy world no object has time to make a deep impression.
>
> —Henry Home, Scottish philosopher

OVERRULING THE OBJECTIONS

The pleasure of retreating begins when you open your mind to it. But first, you'll probably encounter a rush of excuses. Let's look at the most common of these:

- "I don't have time!" Re-read the last chapter. Give time to a retreat, and time will expand. The retreat experience creates *psychological time,* the time that runs parallel to outside time—time devoted to noticing, evaluating, and finding meaning. Psychological time helps you *know* you are in a joyful moment or to admit that what you're doing sucks and needs to be changed. You may go into your retreat feeling time poor, but after you've submitted to the experience, time will come home with you. Go.

- "I don't have the money!" Of all the ways we can replenish ourselves, a retreat can provide the most for the least. You can pack a lunch and spend the day in a natural setting near you. Or check out Jack and Marcia Kelly's book, *Sanctuaries,* to locate a monastery or abbey in your vicinity. Call ahead first, but most of these communities of quiet will welcome you to come for the day—at no charge. But even a room and three meals a day is a pretty affordable luxury. Usually, though, our objections about money have little to do with what's in the bank account, and much to do with our priorities. Can you afford to eat? Retreating is a necessary form of sustenance for introverts, just as social gatherings are for the extrovert. Do we tell our extroverted friends that they can't afford to attend these gatherings? Why the double standard?

- "Other people will object." Yes, they very well may. Or, they might tell you *it's about time* you got away. Our challenge as introverts is to adopt the attitude, based on the introversion assumption, that your need to retreat requires no explanation—it is self-evident. If they argue, have them read this chapter. Of course, our right to retreat does not exempt us from managing our responsibilities, as wonderful as that sounds. By addressing what others need from you *up front,* you'll limit the potential for opposition. So if you do the cooking, buy extra pizzas and make ahead some easy meals. If you run a meeting at work, prepare a coworker to take charge rather than dumping the worry on your boss. A little extra effort will multiply in dividends of peace.

RETREAT DREAMS

Now for the fun part: let's plan your retreat. Retreats can take many forms, and you are the only one who can decide what fits you. One introvert may need pristine natural surroundings; another will savor the anonymity of a large city. Some introverts prefer to have everything provided—meals, maid service—and others prefer being entirely on their own. The retreat options today are as varied as our interests. Here's a partial list:

- Silent retreat
- Wilderness retreat
- Spirituality retreat
- Yoga retreat
- Meditation retreat
- Spa retreat
- Study retreat or sabbatical
- Reading retreat
- Writing retreat
- Adventure retreat
- Poetry retreat
- Shopping retreat
- Artist retreat
- Nature photography retreat
- Vision quest
- Heart-of-the-city retreat
- Beach retreat
- Ranch retreat
- Sailing retreat
- All-inclusive retreat

As you begin to plan your retreat, set practical considerations aside. You can work those in later. You may want to grab a pad and pen, or write your notes right here in the book. It's yours, after all. Now consider the following:

- What is your vision of the perfect retreat setting? Give yourself time to look around in your mind's eye. Take it in. Spend as much time as you wish.

- What do you see as you look around?
- What smells do you notice?
- What are the sounds around you?
- What is the temperature?
- What feelings do you have in this place?

Perhaps you're imagining green grass, rolling hills and a view for miles around. You might see yourself kayaking down a rushing river. Or maybe your haven is a funky café in an artsy village or bohemian borough. Once you choose your setting, think about accommodations:

- How important is interior space to you? Maybe you don't want to go inside at all: you just want to bask in nature and carry your accommodations on your back. Maybe you don't want to go outside at all: you want to lock yourself up with good books or old movies and only open the door for room service. Maybe you want the best of both: a gorgeous interior with a magnificent view or pristine surroundings.
- What interior style do you prefer? Do you envision a sleek, contemporary suite, a cozy cottage with handmade quilts, or a simple beach house with wood floors? Would you like to try something exotic or very different from your own living space?
- How do you like your meals? Would you prefer to have meals included in your package so you don't have to plan? Or would you enjoy having a variety of restaurants nearby to accommodate your culinary whims? Do you want the option of eating in? If so, would you prefer a gourmet kitchen, a fridge you can stock with snacks, good local delivery, or twenty-four-hour room service?

Now that you have a feel for your retreat preferences, let's look at some options. *Retreat centers* usually provide a room and three meals a day, and offer scenic grounds for roaming on your own. The downside is that there are other people around, and meals are usually served cafeteria-style. However, these centers, especially those designed for spiritual reflection, have an ethic of quiet respect for other residents. Everyone understands that you don't want to disturb someone who is meditating or has taken a vow of silence. Aha! An introverted society! Some centers offer classes for self-enrichment and others have spa facilities on hand. If you want a place to yourself, some centers do offer private cottages or cabins.

If you want rustic, you'll need to decide if you want a "catered" rustic experience, with outfitters and guides providing gear, meals, and possibly transportation. A nice option for many is a rustic cabin with the essentials or a B&B in a natural setting. Some introverts prefer an outdoor "room" under the stars and others prefer a cushy bed with books strewn about. If you want something different, rent a tree house, houseboat or *yurt*—the modern version of the nomadic tent.

While some introverts want easy access to natural resources, others enjoy having cultural resources at hand: shops, restaurants, museums, and sources of entertainment. A city retreat can be a wonderful source of anonymity, especially for those of us who become closed-in by the familiarity of small town life. Whether you plan your retreat in the Rocky Mountains or in the heart of Manhattan, identify what resources are most important to you: a rushing stream, a place to view art, anything that feeds you. As with the five items for your room, consider the five essential resources for your retreat.

Once you have your vision and your priorities, consider how much time you want. Sure, you may decide to pare it down, but allow yourself to consider what would be most satisfying. And when you look at your calendar, be honest with yourself: how long does it take you to settle in? Easing into a retreat is like settling into sleep: some of us fall asleep when we hit the pillow; others need more time to settle down.

> I retreat when I'm driving on the freeway, with the music going through me.
>
> —Cecilia, who loves to drive by herself, fast

If we've been under a great deal of stress, you'll need time to downshift. Rather than rushing to get there, allow the trip to help you transition. Feel the gaining distance.

As far as retreat length, just as each of us requires a different amount of sleep, the amount of time we need for rejuvenation will differ.

So now you have your vision, your priorities, and you've thought about time and travel. Okay, you probably haven't sorted everything out yet, which is great because the planning is part of the magic. What you'll want to do eventually is to place your vision beside the realities of your life and see what you can work out. This is where creativity begins.

As a working woman with a young family, I find that vacation time tends to go to family excursions, which I cherish. But this "time off" is not the same as a retreat. The challenge of working out both has led me to many satisfying compromises. Here are some ideas for how to expand your options:

- If you go away for professional training, workshops, or conferences, stay an extra day or two and chill. Conferences are often hosted in attractive places, and you can probably arrange a private alternative to the block of rooms reserved for attendees. When I attended a workshop in Fort Lauderdale, I soaked up every ounce of private time I could, walking among the towering palms, digging my feet into the sand, sipping a mango margarita at a sidewalk cafe. I didn't meet a single soul, but I renewed mine. Bonus: If your employer pays for transportation, you'll just need to cover the extra days of lodging and meals.
- Adding a Friday and Monday to a weekend gives you four good days. Leave after work on Thursday, and you've just given yourself another day.
- For parents, the kids' week at summer camp is a great time for a no-guilt personal retreat. Here's the week you've been looking for! Even if you want to share part of it with your partner, you'll have time for a solo retreat as well.

• Creativity and study retreats or sabbaticals combine getting away with mental stimulation, sometimes for an extended period of time. When these experiences are connected with your livelihood, you may be able to obtain a grant, paid or unpaid leave, or even work it into your job description. Sometimes getting what we want just comes down to asking for it.

Though we all have practical realities to consider, many of the objections we encounter, external and internal, have more to do with fear than with reality. When you turn your retreat vision into a reality, you learn that you *can* retreat, that others can manage, and that it's really not that hard to pull off. You'll wonder what took you so long.

MINI-RETREATS

As your ideas simmer for your big get-away, let's look the kinds of retreats you can take with minimal to no planning—Breath Retreats, Daily Rituals, and Solo Dates.

A *Breath Retreat* is what we usually refer to as a break—a short withdrawal from activity that allows you to slow down and fill up. The pace of your breathing is a great indicator of stress, and a helpful cue to retreat. When your breathing accelerates, your chest tightens, and your heart seems to be beating faster and harder, you are in stress mode. Sometimes stress can be useful, helping us push forward and get the job done. But, more often, stress sucks. We get panicked, we feel like there's no time and we're already behind; we can't think, and life feels oppressive.

Contrary to common wisdom—which, as we've noted, is commonly unwise—we need *more* retreats when we are busy, not fewer. A *Breath Retreat* is the energy bar for the hungry but busy introvert—quick and surprisingly filling. To take a Breath Retreat, just exit whatever you are doing or *not doing* because you're stuck. Get up and leave. Go to a different place—a place like Winnie-the-Pooh's "Thoughtful Spot"—where you can get a new vantage point. You may just want to relax into your breathing, something that keeps going with no effort on your part. Meditation techniques often begin with a focus on the breath. You can bring a notepad or journal with you and write out all the garbage taking up valuable space in your head. Or you can simply look around and notice something new. Watch a pet or the activity of birds, or look out at the patterns made by traffic or pedestrians. After ten or fifteen minutes, you can reenter your routine, motivated by energy from *inside,* rather than pressure from outside.

> I start to feel this pressure in my head, like there's no more room left. When I meditate, I realize "Wait, there's all this room around the thoughts." Meditation puts spaciousness around stress.
>
> —Doug, who uses meditation as a natural antidepressant

A regular daily retreat, or *Daily Ritual,* is a cleansing practice you incorporate into each day, such as meditation or silent reflection, a leisurely walk, or writing in a journal. If the ritual involves an activity, the purpose is not to further a goal, but to open up reflective space. When you work a retreat into your daily routine, it becomes an anchor for your introversion, assuring you that you will indeed have time to yourself—*today.*

I got the idea for *Solo Date* from the "Artist Dates" that Julia Cameron discusses in her classic creativity manuals, *The Artist's Way* and *Vein of Gold.* Cameron assigns Artist Dates as a date with yourself, for at least an hour's duration, doing something "out of the ordinary." You can see a film, stroll through the park, or do anything that fills up your creative stores. Similarly, a Solo Date is an outing with yourself to satisfy some of your introvert cravings. And it is a delicious treat. My favorite Solo Date is to go to a movie in the middle of a weekday, by myself of course. When I started doing this, my therapy practice was across the street from a cinema. I blocked my Friday afternoons, and walked over to catch the earliest showing of a film. Because these are the least attended showings, I sometimes had the luxury of being the only one in the theatre—a private showing!

But what I came to enjoy most was the time just after the movie, when I emerged from the dark into the world. I noticed everything—a leaf rolling across the pavement in the breeze, the sound of a car door shutting—as if I were still viewing the big screen. I practiced stretching out this experience and developed my movie therapy technique, which we'll discuss more in Chapter 18.

Whatever retreats you design for yourself, do them regularly. Protect them. Put them on your calendar and tell others you will not be available during these times. Turn off your cell phone. And melt.

Chapter 9:
The Freedom of a
Flâneur

The spectator is a prince who everywhere enjoys his incognito"
—Charles Baudelaire

I remember the moment I first read the words of Charles Baudelaire. I was recovering from a surgery and enjoying—in addition to the quiet—a video study course on Impressionism. Baudelaire was a French poet associated with this radical artistic movement. When I read his description of the *flâneur* in his essay, "The Painter of Modern Life" (1863), I was dumbstruck: "How did he know? This is *me* he's describing!" For the first time, I realized that there was a word for my favorite preoccupation. As you read this excerpt, you might recognize yourself as well:

For the perfect flâneur, *for the passionate spectator, it is an immense joy to set up house in the heart of the multitude, amid the ebb and flow of movement, in the midst of the fugitive and the infinite. To be away from home and yet to feel oneself everywhere at home; to see the world, to be at the centre of the world, and yet to remain hidden from the world—such are a few of the slightest pleasures of those independent, passionate, impartial natures which the tongue can but clumsily define.*

We have no equivalent word for *flâneur,* or the feminine *flâneuse,* in our language. The literal English translation, "idler or loafer," has little resemblance to Baudelaire's "passionate spectator" and would likely be considered an insult! We name what we value, and we value the movers and the shakers. Here in America, we describe the spectator by what she is watching and by what she is *not*—not a participant.

THE ARTIST'S EYE

For the introvert, as for the *flâneur,* observing is not a fallback position—something we do because we can't participate. We watch because we *want to.* There is something wonderfully grounding about remaining still as others mull about—or mulling about while others remain still. Against the backdrop of the scene, the introvert feels more like an "I." This enhanced subjectivity is just the opposite of the entrainment that pulls us in and renders us invisible. The entrained introvert becomes overstimulated and shuts down; the *flâneur* shops for inspiration and feels larger. It is as if the best parts of ourselves are scattered about. As we stumble upon them in the world, we discover who we are.

The Impressionist painters made this process tangible. They didn't sit in a studio and paint posed models; they walked the streets of Paris and traveled the country, noticing the scenes of modern life and painting what interested them. Recording objective reality was not the goal. Impressionists captured how *they* saw things, and what they saw was better, richer, and more alive than what was out there. This kind of tampering with reality outraged critics such as Albert Wolff, who wrote: "Try to make Monsieur Pissarro understand that trees are not violet; that the sky is not the color of fresh butter." But the Impressionists just got more impressionable: Gauguin and Van

Gogh used shockingly intense (for the time) color pigments to depict a more primal and emotional reality.

Though introverts are drained by interaction, we can take immense pleasure in watching the scene around us: people moving about, their dress, movements, and preoccupations. The Impressionists were masters of people watching. Degas took a special interest in the movements of ballet dancers, but not the performances as much as the process: the stretching, rehearsing, resting. Mary Cassatt, who was not as free to walk the streets due to her gender, painted opera patrons and scenes of domestic life.

> There's a part of me that is always writing the script of what I'm viewing, processing it. Then the muses go to work on it.
>
> —Doug, songwriter, poet, and *flâneur*

In contrast to the "frozen" historical paintings of the time, these artist-*flâneurs* enjoyed recording movement and *change*—whether the changing fashions on the street or the changing light against the cathedral. Series paintings became popular, such as Monet's studies of light—paintings of the same landscape, one at early dawn, another as the scene becomes illuminated, a later version when the sun sets. Pairs of artists, such as Cézanne and Pissarro, would sometimes paint the same scene, revealing how their subjective interpretations distinguished them.

The *flâneur*, artist or not, has a talent for staying *out* of the scene even as he is in the midst of it. This introverted observer can draw energy from society because he or she remains the *interpreter* of what is happening, the integrating action happens inside. This skill—focusing outside while staying inside—can come in very handy. Think of Renoir as he painted his famous *The Ball at the Moulin de la Galette,* and for our purposes, let's assume he's an introvert. Mobs of people are socializing, laughing, drinking, and reveling. It's noisy and chaotic. But Renoir gets to engage in a solitary pleasure amid all of this. He sees the color and the lighting; he gets to choose what story to capture. And he's not bothered or annoyed by the activity—he's a *passionate* observer. And his painting captures his passion. The chaos is beautiful, sparkling with life and vitality.

In our forward-moving, competitive society, it's easy to reduce our focus to the step ahead or the obstacles in our way. We are too much a part of the action—and *interaction*—to *see* what's happening. Yet, *flâneurie* is a wonderful tool for the introvert, whether roaming the city or stuck at a party.

Let's say you're talking to someone—no, someone is talking to *you*—and that person is really enjoying the sound of his or her own voice. You feel trapped and don't have the energy to withdraw. Try playing *flâneur* and look for the artistic, and perhaps comic, value of the situation. I have observed very boring conversations—no, monologues—come to life when I look at the speaker as a work of art: the character lines on his face, the way he or she gestures, the color of her lipstick. For extreme talkers, it usually matters not if we are listening—they just want to talk. (These are the talkers who continue the monologue as we walk away.) Yet, their talking only distances us. Sometimes we can actually feel more empathy when we bypass the talk and look into eyes that are real, or internally narrate a story about the conversation, or imagine what role the talker would play in a movie. If you are cast as the observer, you might as well relish the experience!

AMONG, YET ALONE

As I write today, I am sitting in a Starbucks. I drove an hour to get here, even though I have my pick of coffeehouses ten minutes from my home. I didn't come all this way for the coffee. As you recall, it's the "house" in coffeehouse that attracts me. I came to this particular Starbucks because I don't know anyone here or, rather, no one knows *me*. My identity is invisible. And it is this invisibility that frees me to study my surroundings. Samba music plays in the background, the cobalt blue of low-hanging lamps accents the warm tones of the room, and from my table next to the window, I can watch people in here or out there, strolling, conversing, smoking, or studying.

The introvert who is not broadly known has an advantage. While extroverts talk away, she is free to observe, to think, to enjoy the details and nuances of the situation. Though I love to act and have had my Hollywood fantasies, I can imagine no fate worse than being known everywhere. I recall the scene in the movie, *Lost in Translation,* in which the American actor/celebrity relishes a moment of anonymity at a nightclub in Tokyo, only to have a couple of eager fans proclaim, "You're Bob Harris!" As if he didn't know.

Walking in an unknown city is a delight for an introvert. Unfortunately, American cities have become less walkable. I have yet to live in a neighborhood with sidewalks—these were eliminated as suburbs became "bedroom communities" and malls replaced streetside shops. Edmund White, author of *The Flâneur,* writes, "Americans are particularly ill-suited to be *flâneurs*" because we are so driven to improve ourselves. I would add that being a *flâneur* is difficult because we are so driven to *talk.* Example: you are taking a thoughtful walk, sorting out your feelings after a difficult conversation, and your neighbor calls out, "Hey! Are you coming to the block party?" Or you are browsing a bookstore, feeling that reverence that introverts have for books, and an acquaintance recognizes you before you have a chance to duck around the corner.

> I'm never happier than when I am alone in a foreign city; it's as if I have become invisible.
>
> —Storm Jameson, author of more than fifty novels

We have an assumption here in America that the kind thing to do is to be "friendly," which means being extroverted, even intrusive. The Japanese assume the opposite: being kind means holding back.

So, today I am in the city next door rather than my own. I mentioned to my husband and boys my plan to come here to write and they were thoroughly confused: "Why would you spend two hours driving in order to write?" Anonymity is why. The paradox is, when I travel and am assured anonymity, I feel friendlier. I enjoy my exchanges with the shop owners and even welcome a greeting from someone setting up a laptop nearby. But, really, this makes sense. An introvert just needs time and space, and interaction occurs more spontaneously. But because we get so little time and space, we spend more time defending our boundaries than we do reaching beyond them.

When I sent questions to introverts I knew to be very private, I was surprised by their candid, unselfconscious responses. Cecilia, my contact from Puerto Rico, explained: "Only when we can be guaranteed anonymity, can we take our masks off and bare our souls. When we are no one, we become who we are." As an author, I shouldn't be surprised—I bare my soul quite frequently. I'm just doing it on my time and in my own way.

FLÂNEURIE 101

To learn the art of *flâneurie,* or strolling the city without aim, let's look to the Parisian *flâneurs* for some tips:

- Give yourself a nice, open stretch of time. Vacations are ideal, because you have already cleared the time, and you're likely to be away from what's familiar. But an open Saturday would work just as well.
- Go somewhere new. Explore a new area of the city. If you live in the country or a small town, retreat to a neighboring city for the weekend.
- Leave your goals behind and assume the perspective of the child. Baudelaire captures this attitude: "The child sees everything in a state of newness; he is always *drunk.* Nothing more resembles what we call inspiration than the delight with which a child absorbs form and colour." And White: "He (or she) is a Parisian in search of a private moment, not a lesson, and whereas wonder can lead to edification, they are not likely to give the viewer gooseflesh." Goosebumps are a good sign.
- White suggests staying clear of the tourist centers and monuments—where people are checking off their lists of "Major Sights"—to look instead to the unusual, the "tilting paving stone," and the details that often go unnoticed. This advice reminds me of a city stroll I took with other members of my writers' group. We met up at

6:30 a.m. in our downtown Charleston to find images for a book we were writing. I realized that I had never looked up at the top of the old buildings. I was transfixed as I saw the beauty architects and builders had taken the time to create but I had been too busy to see: elaborate trim, elegant cornices, gargoyles, and even painted art. As we looked upon one building, we saw a large but aging portrait looking out of an upper window: a mystery waiting to be solved. White sees an entirely different Paris than the typical tourist, including some very different museums, such as the Museum of Romantic Life and museums of hunting, eyeglasses, and perfume.

At school, I hide in my drawings. At home, I hide in my room. If it's possible, I like to totally remove myself, like on the roof or in another city.

—Solveig

Today I was thinking I should put back up my hammock on the balcony. It's really soft and I can sit there unbeknownst to my neighbors below. When I had it up, I could watch the breeze move through the trees, or compare which neighbor is the worst car parker, or just see clouds move by.

—Cecilia

YOUR INVISIBILITY CLOAK

Ever wish you could be invisible? If you were, where would you go? What would you look for? What would you like to overhear?

The invisibility fantasy is a popular one for introverts because it allows the possibility of pure observation. Though some of us like to get on stage, many introverts are content to put on their invisibility cloaks and watch. But well-meaning extroverts will have none of that! They need to draw us out, invite us to participate—repeatedly—and question why we are so depressed as to not want to join. Unfortunately, J. K. Rowling has not yet patented a working invisibility cloak like the one her fictional hero Harry Potter found so useful.

Sometimes we can find a private vantage point for observation, like a rooftop, but this option is not likely to be available during the meeting at work or at the local softball game.

In lieu of an invisibility cloak, you might find it useful to have a "prop" on hand, such as a book, journal, or, for some, a sketchpad. These props communicate that you are involved in something and don't want to be disturbed. When I roam to write, I carry a number of props: laptop, bookbag, and purse. My friends call me the "bag lady." Though you needn't carry an entire office, having at least a few props can help you stake out a space and, as Baudelaire put it, "set up house in the heart of the multitude." And even a jacket can serve as a space-expander: put it on the chair next to you and you're less likely to have a "friendly" intruder sit down to talk.

But perhaps we would do best by incorporating *flâneurie* into the American vocabulary and imagination. We can promote safer and more walkable cities. We can stop assuming that just knowing someone is cause for conversation. Perhaps we could don T-shirts with "*Flâneur*" printed on them as a way of signaling the choice to remain anonymous. Sometimes wearing black helps. Or we could pretend we're invisible and just not respond to anyone. But when familiar surroundings and people close in, there's nothing like hopping on the train or into your car and finding a place where you are happily unrecognized.

Chapter 10:
Inroads to Intimacy

*If successful, the link results in a merging of both
minds, essentially creating a single consciousness in
the two bodies.*

— memory-alpha.org

As I read about the Vulcan mind meld in *Memory Alpha,* an
online *Star Trek* encyclopedia, I thought about how convenient
this gift would be for introverts. We could forgo the preliminaries, develop some cue to identify others who wanted to do
the same, and meld away—*no talking required!*

The beauty of the mind meld, as I understand it, is that,
once you meld, you can disconnect, retaining an understanding of the other person. Then you can get to the *real*
conversation. Of course, introverts would require shields to
prevent unwanted intrusion, and would use the mind meld
very selectively, as apparently the Vulcans did. According to
Memory Alpha, "It is a deeply personal thing, part of the
private life, and not normally used on aliens."

Psychoanalysts like Freud and Jung developed their own
techniques for going deep, or reading "unconscious communication," in order to understand and help their patients.

A familiar example is the "Freudian slip," an accidental turn of a phrase that reveals a more honest feeling. Mostly, though, the approach just teaches the therapist to listen on different levels at the same time. Though I was intellectually fascinated by the approach, I think I pursued the training primarily because I wanted to connect. I believed that if I had the whole story, if I had the opportunity to really *know* the person I was sitting with, there would be nobody I could not love. And my idealistic belief found support.

Some clients shield me from access, and I have learned to respect that—I have my own shields, after all. Some I cannot reach—my powers are human, not Vulcan. But the ones who let me in, regardless of how obnoxious they may be on the outside, consistently reveal themselves to be loveable. There's really nothing that mysterious about it: we were all children once, we've all been hurt, and each one of us has a story.

Let's clear one thing up: *Introverts do not hate small talk because we dislike people. We hate small talk because we hate the barrier it creates between people.*

We want less—and more: less talk, more understanding. The ultimate question of a capitalist, "What do you do?" keeps conversation focused on activity rather than on motivation and personhood. If you hate your job, the conversation will have little to do with you. You'll tell the inquisitor what you do, he'll ask more about it, and the conversation will move further and further away from what you value. When I lived in Minnesota, I was known as a psychologist, a smart professional who listened to people. What people did not know about me was that I was also an actor, a slow reader, a theologian who once considered the ministry, that I had a secret wish to go to Paris and study under a chef like Audrey Hepburn did in *Sabrina,* that I was tired of classical music because I heard it so much as a child, that I feared abandonment, that I still found excitement in the bright-colored stories of Betty and Veronica of the *Archie* comics.

Whew! Once an introvert gets going…anyway, when we moved and I left behind my practice, I happily entered a place where I had no identity. I puzzled about how to answer the dreaded question, "What do you do?" I could have easily said that I was a psychologist and then get the standard response, "So, you must be analyzing me." Instead, I decided to just tell the person what I was into that particular day. Some days, I was a general contractor for the crew building our house. Others, I was writing about Eve. Some days, I lingered in my favorite shops. Most days were a mix of a lot of things.

We are all a mix of a lot of things, but conversation generally *reduces* us. So how do we get to the *more* inside? I started to answer this by writing out some alternative conversation starters—an *extroverted* method. But I caught myself, as I do more readily now. For introverts, relationships begin inside.

Let's use the desire-based method we discussed in Chapter 7. Whether you are looking for a friend, love interest, or small community, imagine having exactly what you wish for. Get as specific as possible. These questions may help:

- Where are you? What setting are you in?
- Are you involved in an activity or just hanging out?
- How do you communicate?
- What do you appreciate about this friend or friends?
- What are you learning from the friend(s)?
- What does this friend(s) appreciate about you?
- What feelings do you have when you are together?
- What can you share with this person?
- What passions or interests do you have in common?
- What are your deal-breakers? What characteristics are not acceptable in the friend(s) you choose?

As you build your personal ideal, notice people around you. Play detective and observe what appeals to you and what turns you off. Make note of relationships you witness directly or in stories—film, literature—that you'd like to have in your life. What is the potent ingredient in these intimate connections? I still remember watching the movie *Beaches* when it came out in 1988, and wishing for the kind of friendship the two female characters shared. But what it was, specifically, that I envied, was the fact that the two women mattered enough to each other that they could fight and feel hurt and run away and come back. I had played it safe in relationships.

Some of my colleagues might argue that it's a bad idea to promote fantasy—that wishful thinking can lead to hurt and disappointment. I would agree that hurt and disappointment are quite possible when we seek out what we want, though I also find that people who keep seeking generally find. But I think that the concern about fantasy is based in the extroversion assumption—the idea that we should just get out there and meet people. This kind of advice is so woven into our thinking that we don't question it. *Introverts are not oriented that way.* "Meeting," in the introductions-and-small-talk sense, is not our thing. Incubating the desire *is* our thing, and it works: we get clear about what we want, excited about getting it, and smart about our strategies. Good incubators are often the ones who seem lucky—they happen to be in the right place at the right time. Because the internal activity is not visible to others, the good fortune seems effortless. And, in a way, it is.

Yes, wishful thinking may result in disappointment. But, if you're an introvert, putting what's *out there* before what's inside is a formula for disappointment: your best stuff stays inside, your energy runs out after the initial introductions, you limit your options, you get discouraged, and, all the while, you're not having fun.

But do introverts expect too much? Might we drive someone away with our intensity? True, those of us seeking deeper connection can be intimidating to those who prefer meeting and moving on. Note that, when I say deeper, this not only refers to psychological or emotional depth. Deeper is what we think about in our private experience, whether we contemplate relationships or why the Cubs' Mark DeRosa swung at ball four with the bases loaded in a playoff game. In one of my books on psychotherapy, intimacy was defined as closeness to another person's thinking. As with the mind meld, the therapist attempts to get as close as possible to the meaning things hold to the *client*. In the consulting room, however, this process goes in only one direction. In the relationships we choose, two minds—or hearts or spirits—are trying to know and be known by each other.

So what is it inside you that you want known? What kind of inner life are you looking for in someone else? Whatever that is, the introvert wants to get to it.

Whatever it is, go to it.

INTIMACY THROUGH IDEAS

If you dislike parties, do you really want to meet partiers? If you don't drink, do you want to spend your evening at a bar? We know the answer ("no"), yet parties and bars are often suggested for people looking to meet someone new—especially a romantic somebody. It seems a simple, but often-overlooked alternative, to seek out the minds that interest us.

If your mind is a notebook, writing as you go, take a writing course or join a writers' group. If science is your thing, attend a lecture series sponsored by a local college and hang out for the Q and A sessions: create the conditions for a meeting of minds. Volunteers are needed everywhere, for environmental projects, research, the arts—you name it. Investing in a cause you care about puts the idea first and the social aspect second. If you'd rather just share the silence, join a meditation circle.

But your search is likely to be more refined than that. Sure, you may want to meet a writer, but not just any writer. You

My friend Christopher and I once discussed world religions. Both of us expressed our confusion over their structure and people's willingness to follow. Our conversation ventured deep into the heart of Catholicism, Buddhism, Islam, and several other dominating religions that we felt were insane to follow completely by the rules. It ended up with me emailing several churches and temples to find an answer, and I found most of their responses to be quite inspiring. Our conversations have also ventured into the theory of evolution, world government, life on other planets, and carbon-based matter. We tend to think deeply.

—Solveig, age fifteen

also want someone who shares the values most important to you. And it would be nice if that person enjoyed a form of entertainment you enjoy. And so on.

This is one of the beauties of online profiles. All of the above can be included, and more. Online friends networks and dating sites, like the coffeehouse, are responding to the needs of introverts. We can write, not talk. We can get to the good stuff, and we can press delete as needed.

Whether you meet someone online or live, you'll find a better match if you give room to your desire, and you clarify what you want.

This requires a huge shift away from our proximity-oriented, "love the one you're with" thinking. For extroverts, who enjoy associating, getting to know a lot of people is not a problem—in fact, it's part of the fun. For introverts, who have limited energy for interaction, we need to be more thoughtful and deliberate about whom we meet—which, happily, is what we do best.

But "going for it" is risky. When we acknowledge what we want and apply energy toward it, we face the possibility of disappointment and loss. When I moved from Minnesota to West Virginia, I had my soul mate with me, but I was hungry for some new female friends, a need I had neglected in the past. I experienced my share of disappointment and loss: the extrovert friend(s) who repeatedly brought someone else along to lunch (the more the merrier, and the less intimate) and the introvert friend(s) who didn't have energy for another relationship. But, looking back, these were proximity friends.

No surprise to me now, I met "my people" at a class on memoir writing. I signed up primarily because I'd heard good things about the class and the topic interested me. Again, in retrospect, it makes sense to me that we often meet "the one" when we aren't looking, but are just engaged in what we love. But I didn't meet just one. I recognized one as a columnist I admired. We talked after class—I am bold when it comes to applauding another person's writing—and it was love at first sight. Cindy and I shared the same vision: I was authoring my first book, a desire she also held, and she had a column, something that was part of my vision. We shared an idea, not in a competitive way, but in a reverent sort of way. Since then, Cindy has launched her first book and I secured a column.

The instructor wanted to foster family feelings among us, and scheduled readings at peoples' houses. Sharing our writing gave us that immediate access introverts crave. At one of the parties, I met another woman, a warm, easygoing introvert. Something had felt familiar about her all along, as if we had grown up in the same family. I trusted her, and my trust was well-founded. Though our lifestyles were quite different, we shared a deep commitment to our values and a hunger for truth. Beth is my best friend—and so is Cindy.

During that class, a few of us gravitated together and eventually formed a writers' group. That was about seven years ago. Now we have a name, *The Writers' Village,* and we are writing a book together— a book that brings a piece of each one of us into a mind meld.

> I'm very loyal to my friends, but I don't have tons of people I consider friends. I hang out with a lot of people, but a good friendship is not something that happens very often. The people I'm close with I would do anything for. I value honesty.
>
> —Ben, musician and producer

STICKING IT OUT

Whether you are looking for your people or your person, accept that you may strike out a few times before you hit a home run. It's not easy to lose a relationship that seemed right at first. In fact, it's one of the hardest experiences in life. But unless you allow some relationships to be wrong, you are unlikely to get to the one or ones that are right.

Whatever kind of introvert you are, some people will find you "too much" in some ways and "not enough" in others. You may be considered too intense or not enough into socializing. And when you are seen this way, it hurts. And you question yourself. That's normal.

But it's crucial that you also see the other side of the equation. When you look back on someone who has disappointed you or left you, he was probably "too much" in some ways and "not enough" in others. Maybe he was too much into partying and not enough into closeness. The signs were there all along, but you didn't want to see them, or perhaps they were covered over by the hopes you both had at first. Or perhaps the person came into your life for a reason, and the two of you helped each other through something.

To sharpen your relationship awareness, grab a sheet of paper and a pen. Along the left side, make a list of your past relationships that didn't work. Across the top, list the headings, "Not Enough," "Too Much," and "Gift." Then, for each person, note what was not enough for you, what was too much for you, and a gift you received from that person. If the loss is fresh, feel free to leave the "Gift" column empty—especially if you're still angry and grieving.

As you look over your list, you'll probably see some patterns. Do you tend to draw people who are consistently unable to give you what you need? Or, perhaps you attract people who give you a lot of what you don't need. When you start to become conscious of these patterns, ask for honest feedback from someone you trust, or give yourself the gift of a therapist. By investing the time to figure it out, you'll save yourself time in trial-and-error relationships.

Comfort in relationships is key for introverts, so time is an important factor in existing relationships as well. Sometimes it just takes a certain amount of hanging out together before we feel safe enough to disclose the good stuff. That's why family relationships can be extremely important to introverts. Siblings already share a history, so a lot of groundwork has been taken care of. A partner or spouse can become a safe haven of intimacy in an overstimulating world. Introverts also benefit from knowing others are in it for the long

> *Insanity: doing the same thing over and over again and expecting different results.*
>
> *—Albert Einstein, physicist and novel thinker*

haul. My two sisters closest in age and my husband are the people with whom I have risked the most honesty, and they with me. We know we're not going anywhere and that our closeness is the ultimate goal.

GOING DEEP

So here's where we talk about conversations, because you'll probably have one at some point. If you want a book on icebreakers, this is not it. Icebreakers are usually just silence breakers, and they're usually designed to initiate talk at social events. They can be extremely useful for those purposes, but those are not the purposes we are talking about. Here are some thoughts on how to "go deep" with people you find through your introvert channels:

Don't…

Introduce topics that bore you—i.e., "Where do you work?"

Ask questions that can be answered with "fine"—i.e., "How are you?"

Do…

Ask questions you don't know the answer to—i.e., "When did you first know you wanted to teach?"

Ask for personal definitions—i.e., "Help me understand. When you say the film was 'dark,' what does that mean to you?"

Observe. Notice how it's going. Allow silence. Don't try too hard.

Being authentically introverted in relationships may feel weird at first. That's because, in our society, we equate relating with being extroverted. In the next section, we move into the spaces we share with extroverts, and practice staying where we are.

Part III:
Standing Still in a Loud World

Chapter 11:
The Conversation
Conundrum

The difficulty with this conversation is that it's very different from most of the ones I've had of late. Which, as I explained, have mostly been with trees.
—Douglas Adams

Many introverts find great companions in pets—and trees—because they don't *talk*. When I walk my dog, I can tell her everything on my mind, and she doesn't interrupt; she doesn't top it with a story of her own—she just walks with me. Ah, if people were only so easy. There is probably no area of greater conflict for an introvert than in the arena of social conversation. That is, if there are extroverts involved. Here's an example:

Extrovert: How is your day going?

Introvert: (taking the question in, thinking)

Extrovert: I have had the craziest day…

Introvert: Yeah? (distracted from thinking)

Extrovert: Yeah, it all started this morning when… (continues for five minutes or so) … So you're doing well then?

Introvert: Yeah. Oh, I gotta get going. See ya!

While the introvert is reflecting on the question (thinking first), the extrovert takes this as an invitation to fill the void (talking first). As long as the introvert doesn't interrupt, the extrovert continues to fill the interpersonal space with talk. But as long as the extrovert talks, the introvert can't think and stays mute. Mute means the invitation is still open, and continued talk assures that the introvert remains mute. By the time the extrovert pauses to ask, the introvert's head is pounding and he or she just wants to get out so she can think. The extrovert just assumes the introvert had nothing to say, and moves on.

Not all extroverts converse this way, of course. In her book, *Intimacy and Solitude,* Stephanie Dowrick refers to these "needy, talkative, self-absorbed, and unselfconsciously intrusive" people as "exhausters." Emotionally sensitive introverts tend to attract exhausters, or as I call them "extreme talkers." When I work with extreme talkers in therapy, I give them feedback that if they block me out, they aren't likely to get much help from me. They invariably respond with the request, "Please interrupt me." Though this is not my preferred approach, I have found that they do accept my interruptions and pay attention. And there really is no other way in; these talkers have the uncanny ability to keep pauses just short enough to block any possible response.

Whether I cut in or not, I have learned to keep my mind about me amid the talk. I'll share some tricks of the trade later in this chapter. But outside of my office, I rarely interrupt, and I avoid conversations that require me to do so. Emotionally needy people *need* therapy, and emotionally healthy introverts need to avoid oppressive conversations. This may sound crass, but I make a clear distinction here. For introverts, extreme talk is not cheap at all—it takes a huge toll on us. Besides, our listening doesn't really help the talker! If the talker makes his way into therapy, however, the annoying excess—the part that is caught up in something, refusing to move on—is welcome and becomes the focus of treatment. We all have excess, and even the most reserved introverts can become extreme talkers in therapy. Some are so relieved to finally have airtime that they rush to get everything in while there's time. In Ovid's myth, Narcissus keeps looking at himself in the reflection of the pond because he does not yet *know* himself; therapy facilitates this self-knowledge.

If you get trapped in a conversation with an extreme talker, by all means, cut in—then cut out. Keep in mind that the talker may actually expect this, since he or she gives you no other alternative. Once you exhaust your polite efforts, cut in, say a quick "Gotta go—bye!" and cut out—just walk away. Don't look back. He or she is probably still talking.

You think this is rude? If you were being beaten on the head, would walking away be rude? For introverts, being "talked to death" is very much like being beaten on the head. Some of us end up with migraines, some of us get slimed by the anger spewed in our direction, and most of us feel drained of life energy. Talk can hurt us, and protecting ourselves from harm is not rude.

In contrast to extreme talkers, many extroverts strive for balance in the conversation, or even focus entirely on the introvert. These extroverts often ask direct and specific questions, moving the interaction along in a rhythmic fashion. The introvert, who prefers open-ended questions, may dutifully answer the extrovert—the path of least resistance—while becoming increasingly frustrated and bored. Though the extrovert may feel she's getting to know the introvert, the introvert can easily feel bypassed. Remember the tent analogy? The important activity is inside; the aide outside is answering the questions. By contrast, the extrovert's good stuff is right out where you can see it—so no wonder she assumes the same of the introvert.

My husband is one of these "inquisitive extroverts." By the end of a party, he has spoken to everyone there and seems to discover something interesting about each attendee. I recall one of these parties. We drove together—*big mistake*—and he was still enjoying the party well past my burnout point. Because the host was a friend of mine, I felt comfortable grabbing a book from her bookcase and plopping down in a cozy chair. Ironically, the book was Stephanie Dowrick's *Intimacy and Solitude,* a lovely book that kept me company until I was able to pry my escort away.

Inquisitive extroverts are easy to like and good at gathering information. My husband often updates me on my own family! But I've learned not to go to parent-teacher conferences with him. His interrogatory approach leaves me in the dust, and I either sit stupidly or fume until he catches my death stare and gives me some room.

Regardless of the intentions of the extrovert, the underlying dynamic remains:

- Extrovert outpaces Introvert.
- Introvert either tries and gets tired, or listens and gets tired.
- Extrovert fills the void.
- Introvert gives up, and looks for a way *out* of the conversation rather than a way *in*.

Add more people, and the introvert may not enter the conversation at all.

So how do we make an appearance in these conversations? Do we even want to? Let's look at our first example again, but we'll pry open some space for the introvert's feelings, and turn up the volume:

Extrovert: How are you?

Introvert: (taking the question in, thinking)

Extrovert: I have had the craziest day…

Introvert: *Wait a minute! WHAT ARE YOU DOING? Don't fill the void. I LIKE the void! I need the void to make room for my thoughts. So if you really want to know how I am, leave the void alone until I come up with something. If you don't want to wait, that's cool—just find someone else to talk to. I'm really quite content to be alone.*

Alternatively, in the ancient words of Lao-tzu, as translated by Stephen Mitchell, we might ask:

Do you have the patience to wait till your [my] mud settles and the water is clear?

Can you remain unmoving till the right action arises by itself?

—from the *Tao Te Ching*, or *The Book of the Way*

Waiting for the "right action"—or in this case the "right words"—is what introverts do naturally; but extroverts don't easily let the mud settle. They stir it up! So try as we may, our water does not become clear.

THE RISK OF PLAYING

There will always be those conversations that we just get through. Sometimes both parties are just being polite. But it is important to know that when we nod and allow extroverts to dominate we can pay a price. The extrovert ultimately loses too, but that's another book.

One problem with playing along is that, in the absence of talk, extroverts are easily able to project their own thoughts onto us. *We* know that we're not really present in the conversation, but the extrovert does not know this. To the extrovert, silence is just silence. The void is *devoid.* Or the void is agreement. Or the void is whatever the extrovert needs it to be—not because the extrovert is evil, but because he or she is oriented to external action. It just happens that the only action being recognized is the extrovert's. Let me provide some examples:

- A reporter asks, "So what are your thoughts on the situation?" As you think about it, he continues, "A lot of people are feeling this way..." You nod to indicate that you're listening. He quotes you as saying what he just told you "a lot of people" have been saying. This scenario actually happened to me. Even though I had eventually shared my own thoughts with the reporter, because I nodded and did not actively dispute his statement, he assumed and even quoted my agreement. I read his thoughts, attributed to me, in the newspaper the next day.
- Your extroverted partner talks with you about a problem the two of you need to address. You listen, not sure what your thoughts are on the matter. You may nod to indicate that you are listening. Because you don't say much, your

partner assumes agreement, but you don't follow through on her expectations. Your partner is mad.

In these examples, the extrovert carries away potentially damaging assumptions about you. In one case, you are publicly misrepresented. In the other, a loved one sees you as neglectful or inadequate, or both.

Even though these responses may cause harm, the greatest harm occurs when we start to *take on* the beliefs of the extrovert. This happens very subtly, and we may not even realize what's happening. Though we think we're dismissing the extrovert by providing a patronizing response, we also dismiss *ourselves*. Let's consider the example of you and your partner: he or she brings a specific set of assumptions to the conversation. Your partner assumes something is wrong, and that he or she has a solution. Because you haven't had a chance to think about it, and it sounds pretty good, you go along with it. But then you find yourself, and your partner finds you, not following through on the solution. You and your partner *both* conclude that you are neglectful or inadequate, or both.

But, more likely, you haven't really bought in to your partner's way of thinking, and *this* is why you aren't following through. If you take your partner more seriously, *and* take yourself more seriously, you would need time to explore your own assumptions about the proposed solution. Once you do so, you may discover that you have a whole different take on the situation. You're not a bad person after all—you just have not entered the conversation!

But if you don't take the time to find your own truth and you conclude that you are just a bad person, the harm goes deep. You wonder why you're so negligent, so lazy, so thoughtless—actually, you *haven't* thought enough, you become alienated from yourself, and you're on your way to that self-hating syndrome called depression.

STOP! It is time to stop the conversation, stop the self-reproach, and start tuning in to what you think. When my own psychoanalysis gave me the time to tune in, I was struck by how much I had inadvertently agreed to. After one of my sessions, I wrote this poem, which I titled "I Will Decide":

> You used to soak into my pores
> you infiltrating, me accommodating.
> I became your wants and needs
> I became you.
> I used to disappear into your opinions
> My head nodding, my "uh-huh" echoing
> You represented me.
> Then I woke up
> A neonate, but with a powerful cry,
> "I am mine, and I will decide."

SLOWING IT DOWN

So how do we stop the action, or at least slow it down, so that we can let our mud settle and discover our thoughts?

The answer is simple, but challenging: **Hold your ground.** Notice that I didn't suggest you think of a witty retort: we suck at that. Holding is very different than responding. Holding your ground means doing whatever you need to do to stay centered. In this sense, it is a kind of meditation, a practice in stillness. For some of us, this means holding your *head* steady, resisting your tendency to nod and say "uh-huh." Let your face show that you don't know yet. Tune in to what you are feeling. Your head may trick you, but your gut is usually dead-on.

Holding your ground also means staying free of the pressure to entrain, to succumb to the spell of extrovert intensity. Social skills training stresses the importance of eye contact, but limiting eye contact may be necessary when you need to unlock from the gaze of an intense extrovert.

Psychoanalytic therapists learn to maintain a position of neutrality so that the client remains free to express himself. For introverts, maintaining neutrality is a way to remain uncommitted until you have an opinion or response. This skill takes discipline. When someone is laughing and you don't find it funny, you don't laugh. When someone says, "You know what I mean?" and you don't know what she means, don't say "yeah." You don't even need to say "no," because the question is rhetorical. Doing nothing is amazingly powerful.

As you wait for your mud to settle, notice what's going on inside you. Turn up the volume on your internal voice. For a psychoanalytic therapist, the inner voice helps lead to insight about the client. For example, when I am bored by something the client is saying, that is an indicator to me that the client is stuck in a neurotic repetition—same story, different day. My boredom tells me that the client is avoiding something.

In the case of a casual conversation, your inner voice is for *your* use. Here's an example:

Extrovert: We need to talk.

Introvert: Silent. (Thinking: "Why?" "I don't feel a need to talk.")

Extrovert: We aren't spending enough time together.

Introvert: What do you have in mind? (shifting the discussion from "we" to "you"; getting more information)

Extrovert: I want you to be around more.

Introvert: Silent. (Thinking: "Noooooooo! I don't get enough time to myself as it is!")

Extrovert: Why aren't you saying anything?

Introvert: (Honest) Because I'm thinking about what you're saying.

Extrovert: So what do you think?

Introvert: (Puzzled, internally-focused look) I'm thinking a lot of things (slowing it down).

Extrovert: (Impatient) *Well?*

Introvert: Let's see (slowing it down). I want to respond to you, but I'm also worried.

Extrovert: About WHAT?

Introvert: Silent. (Thinking: "Back off! Why are you so mad?")

Extrovert: (The silence amplifies the extrovert's overreaction.) Okay, sorry. Go on.

In the example, the introvert stays silent when the question requires a betrayal of self. The introvert also talks at the pace of his or her emerging thoughts and feelings. I am reminded of the game show, *Who Wants to be a Millionaire?* As contestants on the show search for the right answer, they are encouraged to talk through the process. By bringing the internal process out, they are better able to focus on their thoughts—rather than on external pressures like television cameras and the clock.

Introverts, you have a right to remain silent. You have a right to not know. You have a right to ask for more information. We'll talk more about caring for intimate relationships in Chapter 15, but remember that many conversations are optional, and that most conversations can be postponed until you feel more up to it. Here are some other tips for making space in conversations:

- Look down—or sideways or up—as a way of temporarily unlocking from the expectant gaze or flow of words directed at you. Show that you are thinking by furrowing your brow, scratching your head, or whatever body language comes most naturally to you.
- Work in a break. If someone asks a hard question, say, "That's a hard question. I want to sit with it a bit. Let me shoot you an email later." If you can't think of anything, say you need to hit the restroom. It's not a lie. You do need a rest!
- Pick your medium when you can. If someone says, "I'll give you a call" and you detest phone conversations, say "Could you email me instead? I'm harder to reach by phone." Even if you answer all your calls, this is not a lie: you *are* more defensive and harder to reach in a phone conversation.
- Give *yourself* a break. There will be days where you will forget all of this, or you'll just be too tired to try. Like meditation or physical exercise, this is a *practice,* not a test you either pass or fail.

- Give yourself second—and third, and more—chances. If you think you betrayed yourself in a conversation, and you will, you have the right to go back and edit what you said. My kids don't like when I do this and will protest, "But you *said...*" I just hold my ground and say, "Yes, I did say that. Now I'm saying this."

CONVERSATION PREPARATION

The most terrifying experience of my life, other than jumping out of a plane, was taking unscreened phone calls on a live television news show. The clock was ticking—it was a four-minute segment—and callers often asked questions that would take about a year or three of therapy to answer. Slowing things down was not an option. When I jumped out of a plane, I at least had a parachute to slow my fall!

There are some conversations that cannot be slowed down. A job interview needs to cover a lot of ground in a limited time frame, and media interviews barely give you time to introduce yourself. If your words aren't ready at a moment's notice, you may lose an important opportunity. Though quick responding is not the introvert's forte, you can nail these forums by preparing. Consider this: most authors (as well as many actors) who provide media interviews are introverts. The secret is to practice these conversations before you have them. Here's how:

- Find someone you feel comfortable with to play the interviewer. Have him or her shoot you questions, get stumped, fumble and flub, get over it, get it together, and get through it, over and over again.
- Take a break between each practice session and think about what you want to say. Jot down and memorize a few key points that you want to cover. Keep it as simple as possible: you just need some ideas to get the ball rolling. You'll be able to take it from there.
- Have your practice interviewer change his or her questions so that you get flexibility training.

- As you practice, ask for feedback or videotape your responses to see how you come off. Recall the metaphor of the general in the tent? If you tend to keep your genius inside and send an aide to do the talking, you'll want to make sure that aide is well trained.

Though some interview situations are high pressure by definition, we can often make formal conversations more introvert-friendly. Consider the following:

- With media interviews, indicate that you'd like to provide "talking points" or a list of questions to help the interview run smoothly. Most hosts appreciate this.
- Do your homework. Listen to the show, talk to the producer about what to expect, Google the people who are interviewing you for the job. Don't let your imagination run wild and scare you. Get the facts.
- Call the shots. I have asked interviewers to send me questions in advance, I have told newspaper reporters that I need to think on a question and get back to them, and I have said "no." You often have more power than you realize.
- Remember that you know more about you—your research, your qualifications, your opinions—than anyone else in the room.

Another pressured conversation that deserves mention is the doctor visit. Doctors, especially those working for an

When I was sixteen or so, I had the dreaded session with the school's guidance counselor. I remember…answering her questions with my trademark short and quiet answers. After about five minutes of this she said to me, "Why don't you look me in the eye when you talk to me?" She really caught me off guard as no one had ever called me on that before. Frankly, I had never realized I did that. I have never forgotten that conversation. It seems obvious, I'm sure, to most people, but from that day on I started looking at people when I talked to them. It actually helped me…feel less alone.

—Ingrid, day job: internal auditor; passions: travel, reading, wildlife (to name a few)

HMO, are characteristically rushed. How many times have you had your head filled with questions for the doctor, only to come up blank when he or she asks, "Anything else?" The doctor is halfway out the door, you can't think, so you answer, "I guess not." Then, the minute you get home, a flood of questions comes back to you, and you want to kick yourself.

Or you've hired a lawyer or accountant, and you *pay* for your conversation, so short is indeed sweet. In these cases, it helps immensely to write down what you want to cover; tell the doctor (or lawyer or accountant) at the beginning of the appointment that you have a list. After all the school they've gone through, they know how to complete assignments, and the written word carries power. And professionals are concerned enough about *their* lawyer's fees to see to it that your list is attended to.

MUSIC TO OUR EARS

The conversations that are free of conundrums are the ones, usually with another introvert, in which there is plenty of time for the mud to settle, and for clarity to come. These are the conversations that lead to discovery—of self as well as the other. They happen with extroverts, too, but require more commitment and effort. The yin-yang conversation between opposites in love can generate amazing insight and growth—that is, if you can both stand it. We'll indulge in these more rewarding conversations in Chapter 15.

Chapter 12:
The Anti-Party
Guide

At every party there are two kinds of people—those who want to go home and those who don't. The trouble is, they are usually married to each other.
—Ann Landers

If we wanted to sort introverts from extroverts without the help of the MBTI®, we could just send everybody to a party and note what time each person leaves. A party is one activity that seems to polarize introverts and extroverts. Extroverts love them; introverts avoid them. Introverts may enjoy a party—for a little while—but will start looking to the exits long before the extroverts come up for air. And, even though more than half of the population would rather stay home with a book or a close friend, our society equates party with *"fun!"* Tell someone you don't particularly enjoy parties, and you might as well say, "I'm no fun."

Though many of us freely admit to our anti-party senti-ments, many of us also secretly wonder if we are "party poopers"—people who are not only un-fun, but also spoil the fun for others. If you want evidence for society's extroversion assumption, just tell an extroverted friend that you don't want to go to the party or, if you're there, that you want to go home.

> I have friends who don't understand that when I want to leave a party, I really want to leave. Their pleading with me to stay is not going to change my mind. They may want to socialize all night, but I don't!
>
> —Ingrid, who has much more fun at home

First of all, unless your friend is unusually enlightened, she probably won't believe you. The extroversion assumption says, "Everyone wants to go to the party." Secondly, she will probably interpret your reluctance as shyness or a need to feel wanted. The extroversion assumption says, "Because all people want to go to the party, a refusal means that the person needs encouragement." So the extrovert freely encourages you: "You *have* to stay! It's just getting good! You've only been here two hours! Don't be a party pooper!"

Would a friend as freely pressure you into helping her clean her kitchen? An introvert may actually prefer this option, because the two of you could at least talk in a quieter, less pressured setting. But, unless he or she is a *really* close friend, such an invitation would be considered an imposition. Not so with the party. Parties are fun!

It is hard for extroverts to understand how truly oppressive a party can be for an introvert. See if this sounds familiar:

You have come to this party because a friend insisted. The friend who talked you into coming spent five minutes with you and introduced you around a bit. He is now heartily mingling. You do not know anyone else very well, and you've participated in as much small talk as you can stand. It's too early to leave gracefully, so you linger at the snack table for a bit, make a call on your cell, spend a little extra time in the bathroom, and, if all else fails, drink heavily. You feel trapped. You have no interest in working your way into a banal conversation (unless perhaps you chose to drink heavily); you don't want to look pathetic by shadowing your friend; and sitting alone would look downright pitiable—besides, there's no place to sit! Your energy level is taking a nosedive, and you just want to go home, change into sweats, and turn on some good music. Help!

A situation like this—especially if you are dependent on an extrovert for a ride—resembles some forms of torture, such as forced sleep deprivation. In both cases, you are trapped in a state that becomes increasingly painful to maintain. It's an extreme comparison, I know, but most introverts know what I'm talking about. By contrast, many extroverts have absolutely no clue what we go through. And even the more empathic extroverts, and even *introverts,* are not socialized to question the universality of the "Party equals Fun" equation.

So we question ourselves: "Why can't I be more fun? Why don't I *have* more fun? Everyone else is having a great time! What's wrong with me?" This self-alienation is a part of the torture. If you felt alone in your desire to leave, you feel *alien* when you scan a room full of laughing, smiling partiers. I'm one of those introverts with well-honed social skills, and I have even danced on the occasional table, but I have felt sheer panic when my exhaustion precedes my exit. It's like the Cinderella story with a twist: I *want* to get out of there and into my duds before midnight—or ten, or eight.

Now an extrovert, or even your therapist, might suggest that if you're stuck, "just make the best of it" and join in. Let's get this straight: *making the best of it and joining in are mutually exclusive at this point in the game.* Why? Because whatever small ration of energy you have left will be consumed by such an effort. Deep down, you know this, which is why you remain frozen at the fringes, even as you tell yourself you really should join in.

Fortunately, there *are* ways we can make things better. And they won't involve acting like an extrovert. Remember, your power source is introversion. Let's look at how to drink in some of *that*.

"No" Is an Option

Yes, saying "No" is an option.

"Thanks, but no."

"No thanks."

"Hell, no."

Whatever works for you, it's your option.

Though this two-letter word is the simplest and clearest response, it's not easy for many of us to say. Why? Because, according to the prevailing extroversion assumption, inviting you is a nice gesture, and pressuring you is a compliment—an indication that you are wanted. How many times have you equivocated on or even declined an invitation, only to be asked again—and again?

So, if your friend is being nice, you certainly don't want to look a gift horse in the mouth and say "no!" That would be rude! Out of curiosity, I looked up the gift horse proverb. The gist of it is: if you are given a horse as a gift, just be grateful; don't scrutinize the horse by looking at its teeth—an indicator of the horse's age and value. In other words, take it "as is," and be grateful.

But just as receiving a horse is a problem if you have no room for it, the offer of a party is a burden for many introverts. So if your friend knows you at all, she is being rude by pressuring you to do something that is bad for you. Yes, *bad for you*. Engaging in a painful activity that leaves you feeling crummy about yourself is self-destructive. But your friend is probably not a jerk—you wouldn't have chosen her for a friend if she were. She's just following the social rules. And you may be following them too.

I have certainly caught myself supporting the extroversion assumption as I decline an invitation, feigning disappointment and loser status: "Darn, that sounds *so* fun, but I have plans that night/am swamped with work/need to take care of my sick dog." These responses come so automatically that we may not even realize how misleading they are. We convince others that we are truly disappointed, thereby assuring continued invitations. We even do this with close friends! This finally sunk in for me when my best extrovert friend invited me, for a second time, to a "can't miss" annual Halloween costume party. I smiled and said to her, "That's an introvert's idea of hell." She smiled back and said, "Really?" I said, "Yep.

Especially if it's big, and I don't know very many people." She said, "Yeah, there'll be a lot of people there. You won't want to go."

Though many introverts struggle with the "gift horse" problem, we may also avoid "no" out of FOMO, or Fear Of Missing Out. We worry, "What if I'm wrong? What if I'm really missing out on something I would love?" Add all the party propaganda coming our way, and our FOMO gets us to go "just this once" to check it out. After going just this once to every social event in town, you make the "A" list and have sealed your reservation in hell.

If you cringe at the idea of going, avoid the long detour home that is the party, and say "no." Yes, you'll miss out. You'll miss having to meet people you'll never talk to again. You'll miss being cornered by the party's extreme talker. You'll miss working overtime without pay. And you'll miss out on the alienation and self-reproach that come hand-in-hand with *trying* to have a good time.

But while "just say no" campaigns sound good, they are often unhelpful when it comes to real life situations. The challenge is to take the clarity of NO and adapt it to the invitation conversation. Let's look at an example:

> Extrovert Friend: Hey, my friend Jane and her husband are having a party this weekend. Their parties are always great, and they're going all out this year. You should come!
>
> Introvert: Hmm, I don't think so. (The introvert is thinking, appropriately cautious, and slowing the pace of the conversation.)
>
> Extrovert: Oh, come on. You'll have a great time!
>
> Introvert: You see, I'm different from you that way. That kind of event is not that fun for me. (changing a universal assumption to a subjective, individual one)
>
> Extrovert: Oh, but this is different than a lot of the lame parties in town...

Introvert: But that's just the problem. The more "successful" the party, the less I'm likely to enjoy it.

Extrovert: Okay, now I'm totally confused. (good—you've deconstructed the assumption)

Introvert: I can see why you'd be confused. When it comes to parties, you and I are probably opposites: you like them big and stimulating. I don't like parties very much in general, but the ones I like are small and intimate.

Extrovert: (at this point the extrovert may get it, or may push harder) That's too bad. I was really hoping you'd go with me.

Introvert: That's sweet of you, but think about it: you won't want to hang with me all night. You'll want to talk with everyone, and as you mingle, I'll feel abandoned.

Extrovert: I would never do that!

Introvert: That's not my point. I think it's great that you enjoy talking to so many people! It's just not my thing. If I spend time with you, I like you all to myself. It is not fair for me to expect that of you at a party, and it's not fair for you to expect me to mingle.

Extrovert: Hmm, that makes sense.

This kind of conversation is easier one-on-one, especially with a close friend. But it can also be hard for a good friend to realize that something he enjoys is no fun for you. Your friend has a right to feel whatever he feels about it, but that doesn't mean you need to change how *you* feel. Introvert-extrovert friends often negotiate compromises once these differences are acknowledged. It is one thing to go to a party to help out a friend who needs you and appreciates what it means for you to go. But it's another, much harder, thing to go under the oppression of an assumption that excludes you.

As in the example above, saying no to a friend can be the beginning of understanding. Some friends may admit that they don't really like parties that much either. Once you start challenging the extroversion assumption, it will start to crumble all around you. You may be surprised at the anti-party sentiment that others had been keeping at bay.

But what if the person inviting you is not a close friend, and you don't really want to get into it? You may still want to do a little introvert activism and tell the person that you don't enjoy large gatherings, but appreciate that he or she thought of you. If you want to get to know that person better, you could suggest getting together for lunch instead.

If you just want to get out of it, there's always the introvert backup: "other plans." Be prepared for an intrusive extrovert to inquire about your plans. You don't have to honor the question: just look at the person as if you are sure you heard him wrong (the "surely you didn't just ask me to explain what I'm doing" look) and go on as if he truly did not ask.

Regardless of the situation, adopting the introversion assumption will help. If we assume introversion, we can assume, "Parties are generally disappointing and stressful, and there are loads of better options." It will take discipline and practice to resist the knee-jerk impulse to apologize and/or defend your reasons for not going. Stay somewhere between "No way in hell" and "I *hate* that I've got plans that night—it sounds so fun!" Acknowledge the good intentions of the person inviting you, and then decline without equivocation.

> I prefer to interact with people one-on-one. Any more than that, and the dynamic becomes competitive and then I get bored easily when I'm not directly participating in the exchange. I have fought this for years, feeling it was more "polite" or appropriate to chime in with pieces of my mind. Not anymore. I'm fine sitting back and letting others try to outshine each other.
>
> —Suzanne, paralegal by day, who would rather spend her downtime reading, crafting, painting, writing, running, walking, or shopping—*alone*.

PROS AND CONS

What if you have mixed feelings about going? There is a great deal of variability among introverts and among parties: some introverts have a lot of extrovert in their personalities, and some parties have introvert appeal. Get the information you need to make an informed choice. Look at these factors:

- *How big is the party?* Get a guesstimate on how many people are expected. As a general rule, more people will mean more energy drain.
- *What is the setting for the party?* An indoor party in the middle of winter will probably feel more confining than a summer party on somebody's farm. Consider the people-to-space ratio. Are there places to hide out and be alone? Are there places to sit? Can you easily take a walk?
- *Do you know most of the people there?* This is a huge factor for introverts. A party of intimate friends is a completely different animal from the "meet and greet" type of party. The fewer people you know, the more oppressive the party will be. And even if you know people, do you know them well enough to cut past the preliminaries? Will introverted friends be there?
- *Is there something to do other than talk?* The worst parties for introverts are in uncomfortable and confined settings, where the only options at hand are to talk or to stand and watch other people talk.
- *How easy will it be to leave?* Here's another biggie. If there is a lot of ceremony involved, it may be very difficult to extract yourself without seeming rude.

In addition to the party setup, you'll want to consider the person inviting you. There are good reasons to attend even the worst kind of party, like when your boss invites you, or when your partner really wants to take you, or when your extroverted friend just got dumped by his girlfriend and needs the party *and* you. But even in these cases, there is often room for negotiation.

ESTABLISHING YOUR TERMS

The toughest party situations usually have to do with work. If your boss tells you to go, it's probably a good idea to go.

It helps to be clear in your own mind that this event is *work,* and to think about the role you are being asked to play. If your company is hosting a party, see if you can volunteer to help out, preferably *behind* the scenes. This will give you something to do other than talking and will also impress your boss. Of course, playing bartender or running for supplies may not be an option if you're a high profile employee. If your job is to mingle, think of yourself as an actor, playing your work role while reserving a part of yourself to observe and narrate the situation. But be clear with yourself: the party is work, and does not count as your weekend entertainment!

What about a party that is really important to a loved one? Here are some negotiating points to consider:

- Introvert time. You'll need downtime to restore your energy. How will you get that? If you're a couple with kids, your spouse may agree to entertain the children the next evening so you can have the house to yourself. If you know you won't get enough one-on-one time with your date, work that in too. Making an appearance and going out afterwards can be a nice compromise.
- Driving arrangements. Drive separately, agree on a departure time, arrange to leave early with another introvert, or have your date spring for cab fare home.
- Establish a "no abandonment" rule. If your partner or friend really wants you along, he or she can also *be* a friend by staying with you or "checking in" if you mingle separately, and by taking "breaks" with you for one-on-one activity or conversation. You can even establish nonverbal signals to communicate your status, such as "break," "bored," and "done."

There are rare circumstances that may call for a full immersion in the party scene in the name of love. When a dear extroverted friend of mine was reeling after a tough breakup, I accompanied her to a huge, high-end party that I would not otherwise be caught dead attending. My only reservation was the cost, which she happily covered for both of us. I stayed by her side, endured the numerous introductions, helped her snub her ex, who was also there, and eventually got out of the way when she met up with a former love interest of hers. As they danced, I took a long walk in the moonlight, sat on the hillside, made a couple of calls on my cell, sat in my Miata and looked up at the sky. I checked in on my friend between these excursions, and even accompanied her to the after party—the dance partner was also headed that way. I stayed until I assessed that she was in good hands, and finally drove home sometime before dawn. I knew my presence meant a lot to her, and I didn't carry away an ounce of resentment.

INTROVERTING AT THE PARTY

If you decide to go, be a good friend to yourself and stick with your introversion. Here's how:

- *Plan your escape.* Before you go, develop your exit strategy. If your date or friend has agreed to leave early with you, have a backup plan. Agreements can break down—your friend falls in love, your partner gets a chance to talk to an important contact. Work out *in advance* how you'll get home if "Plan A" fails. If you are not driving separately, have a taxi service or friend or both on call, phone number programmed into your cell. Bring money. Also think through how to escape confining conversations and how to leave unfashionably early. You can always ask a friend or family member to call at a certain time and "need you."
- *Be a flâneur.* This approach is best suited to a large party with mostly strangers. Bringing a notebook, camera, or sketchpad will establish a boundary and vantage point for observation. Pretend you're invisible and walk among people without trying to engage. Being comfortably alone at a party communicates confidence; trying too hard to

engage actually puts you in a weaker position. If you're in someone's home, study the artwork and bookcases; look through picture albums and coffee table books that have been placed out. Use the party as artistic material.

- *Bring your cell phone.* A cell phone is an automatic excuse for privacy. There doesn't even have to be anyone on the other end! You can dictate a story about the party into your voice mail at home.
- *Go for a walk.* A walk in the fresh air can help restore your energy. To avoid having a search party looking for you, let your escort or host know you're stepping out for a bit but will be back.
- *Find an animal or child.* Play with the family pet or rock a baby as the mom mingles. These less verbal companions can provide comfort while meeting a need.
- *Find an introvert.* See if you can identify the introverts in the room. By consciously looking, you will notice people who are bored, off somewhere else in their minds or trying to convince a friend that it's time to go. You'll see people sneaking out early. Look to the fringes of the party and in the shadows. If you find someone who looks as lost as you feel, risk saying "hello" and perhaps, "are you as bored as I am?" You may have found a friend.
- *Be real.* If you want real, be real. You don't have to keep small talk small. You can be polite without selling out. You can acknowledge someone without grinning from ear to ear. Let your depth be evident in your manner, and the people you meet will actually meet *you.*

The challenge of maintaining your integrity as an introvert in the context of a party can actually be a strengthening experience. But then again, so can walking on hot coals. Know what you're getting into, get out before you burn out, and congratulate yourself for making it through.

Chapter 13:
Why Did I Want to
Work with People?

I don't want to achieve immortality through my work...I want to achieve it through not dying.
—Woody Allen

Introverts spend a lot of time pondering the big questions. Our love of ideas often inspires us to pursue noble work. But, as we soon find, these jobs don't pay us for sitting in a soft chair and thinking big thoughts. Once on the job, we discover—to our horror—that we are expected to *carry out* the big ideas, and that usually means talking to PEOPLE. Usually, by the time we discover this, we are up to our ears in debt—not just for the student loans, but also to our own ideals.

Of course, at some level we knew we'd be working with people, whether as clients, customers, or coworkers. But we were having so much fun *studying* the ideas that we put off that reality. Time to look at that dreaded question, "What do you DO?"

DOING VERSUS THINKING

It is typical of our extroverted, externally-oriented society that we define ourselves by what we *do* rather than what we *think and feel.* "Doing" is the observable part and, for many of us, says very little about our work. If you were to observe me in a psychotherapy session, much of what I do is hidden: listening, integrating ideas, looking for patterns, and searching my own experience for empathic links. Most of the statements I make in a session result from a complex internal process. Likewise, much of my internal process remains hidden but forms a foundation for my overall understanding.

For introverts, the *ideas* behind the work are what matters most. We like to produce and create too, but we know that there is always "more than meets the eye." This is why it is sometimes hard for introverts to find words: we really hate to compromise, and words are always a compromise. And if words are a compromise, *work* is often a big fat disappointment.

> All paid jobs absorb and degrade the mind.
>
> —attributed to Aristotle

Like many introverts, I was drawn to my field because I loved the learning of it: exploring the mysteries of the mind and its mechanisms, understanding and developing theories to make sense of it all, and applying what I learned to my own psychology. I'm not sure when it hit me—when it really sunk in—that my focus would necessarily be reduced and impeded when the work became interactive.

Though we also learn through our interactions, introverts *prefer* to learn through independent analysis. Leave us alone and we'll figure it out. But how much time do you get at work to be alone and figure it out, without interruption? What if your job is interactive? How well does the work you wanted match up with the work you have?

WHAT IS WORK?

When we work, we expend energy in exchange for some kind of reward. I find it helpful to distinguish two different kinds of work: Natural Work, the work you are compelled to do because of who you are, and Imposed Work, the work that is hard not only inherently, but also because you have to push yourself to do it. For me, working through conflict with my husband is the former; it takes energy and can be quite difficult, but nobody has to tell me to do it. I hunger for the intimacy and understanding that such work generates. I hunger for *him*. Nobody could *stop* me from doing this work. This is Natural Work.

Another kind of Natural Work I do is writing. It takes energy, sometimes it is extremely hard, and sometimes it takes everything I have. But I am compelled. I have filled journal after journal, voluntarily, since I was a young child. I *need* to write. I love books: the feel of them—they are sacred to me. And *words!* Searching for the "just right" words is worth an exhausting journey; finding them, whether they are mine or someone else's, is like holding something precious and delicate—a rare jewel, a newborn baby. I love everything about writing: the paper, the pens, the desk and drawers. I love it even when I hate it, just as I love my husband even when I hate him.

When you start to look at your Natural Work, you'll probably find many examples in your own life. We are compelled to have babies, even though they ask much more than they can give. We are compelled to create and invent and tackle the mysteries of life. Use the following questions to help you identify your Natural Work:

- *What is your greatest gift?* Your gift is something you may not think much about, because it comes easily for you. You would probably do it whether you were paid for it or not. But it is not easy for everyone. Others may marvel at your gift because for them it is a mystery, something they can't imagine doing. Are you indulging this gift through your work?
- *When do you feel "in your element"?* Some call it being *in the flow*. I call it that "sweet spot" where work and play intersect. You are present, engaged, and free of conflict.

What do you do naturally? Do you attend to the details others neglect? Are you good at making difficult concepts understandable? Do you secretly love to clean? Do you chart out everything on paper without even thinking about it? Get input from the people closest to you, and ask family members what you were "into" as a child. Pull all of this together, and write a job description, outlining the Natural Work you engage in, paid or unpaid, mundane or profound. Can you identify a theme? Perhaps your nature compels you to create beauty, to find solutions, or to heal the suffering. See if you can come up with a title to capture the essence of this work. Are you a "Truth Seeker," a "Nurturer of Life," a "Freedom Promoter"? What is your core purpose or priority?

In America, we don't talk much about what is at the core. We talk about the "top priority" and the "bottom line." We talk about goals and ends rather than constants. Introverts have access to something much more stable—and powerful. That is, if the Imposed Work doesn't pull us off center.

> When I worked at the hospital on the post-op unit, I would have about six patients per night. The amount of energy and courage it took for me to walk in and introduce myself to the patient and usually family members was sometimes overwhelming. The first time I had to do it in nursing school was terrifying. I just had to FAKE it.
>
> —Margit, who knew she'd be a good nurse because of her capacity for empathy

Imposed Work, like Natural Work, takes energy and can be difficult. But on top of this, Imposed Work involves the work of defying nature—the work of pulling yourself up, pushing yourself forward, playing a role. The tricky thing is that, for introverts, we seek out Natural Work and often end up with Imposed Work.

Some introverts hit the right career on the first try, but many of us find work disappointing at first. We may pursue work for practical reasons or because we are good at something, or because we have a compelling vision of what the work will mean. I pursued psychology, because I love analysis. The courses were fascinating, and I was compelled by the mystery of it, just as I am compelled by the mysteries of spirituality and the mysteries of love. I find it both challenging and comforting to explore fields that I cannot master. Looking back, I hadn't really imagined myself providing *therapy.* I liked the *idea* of therapy, but I didn't consider the immense amount of Imposed Work involved: meeting the clients, diagnosing, keeping records, translating session content into a language insurance companies could understand. The "paid job," as Aristotle noted, was degrading to my ideals.

This conflict is particularly tricky for Accessible Introverts. We go into people work because we can see within people: the nurse or physician sees the rich complexity of the body; social scientists see the complexity of the mind and human behavior. But we can't just go right in, and we often work with—and *for*—people who do not share our fascination with the subject.

I see this frustration among introverts in the environmental field: they are compelled to support and nurture what is natural, but end up doing the Imposed Work of fighting *human nature:* lobbying for policy change, schmoozing supporters. They spend much of their time working *against,* pushing and promoting, when what they love about nature is that it *works together* and evolves organically. When we were kids, my older brother—now a doctoral-level fisheries biologist—practically lived in the woods. He thrived on the richness of nature and eagerly memorized the genus and species names of every animal in the thick reference book that became his bible. Now he spends much of his time in an uphill battle to restore what worked best in the first place. He does get to work outdoors, restoring rivers, but much of his work is indoors, in meeting rooms, with people.

But the frustration of Imposed Work is not specific to any field. The introverted engineer with a natural affinity for building may be frustrated by having to deal with the environmentalist! What we share as introverts is the love of ideas and the desire to explore them with minimal interruption. We want and need *input,* but we'd rather get it through reading, research, and rich conversation than through unfiltered talk.

As you go through your workweek, make note of when you are in Natural Work and when you are pulled into Imposed

Work. You might even want to put an "N" or "I" in the margins of your day planner or try to estimate the ratio of Natural to Imposed. Then consider how you might alter that ratio in favor of Natural Work.

Though we care the most about Natural Work, sometimes we get in our own way, buying into society's elevation of form over substance. I have two jobs, author and psychologist, and my workweek is split between the two practices. So what do you think gets pushed aside for a doctor appointment or errands? Well it used to be my writing time—that is, until I recognized how little respect I was giving the work I love the most. I don't like to cancel clients, but I have become just as reluctant to cancel myself, so I compromise and treat both equally. If a client is at a turning point, I'm more reluctant to interrupt that process. If it's deadline week for my writing, I do not see clients and they don't plan to see me.

It is only in the past year that I've talked to my clients about my writing. It has made my life so much easier to have their understanding, to have them know what "deadline week" means. They don't always like it, but I think they like having a therapist who is finding success as an author, and I think they benefit from seeing me practice what I preach.

It is not only good for us to honor our Natural Work. It is our *responsibility.* Look for that "sweet spot," and expand your time there. Once you get out of your own way, though, you'll have another challenge.

A CULTURE OF INTERRUPTION

While Accessible Introverts often do "people work," Shadow Dwellers are more likely to find careers that allow more solitary work. And whether the profession requires crunching numbers or molding a sculpture, the introvert wants to concentrate on the work at hand. The introvert may ask questions or provide input, but would prefer to do so without the fluff of excessive talk. The introvert at work wants to work!

But even the introverts who have the luxury of sticking to their Natural Work are victims of all the Imposed Work associated with the extroverted culture of the American workplace. Walls have come down and cubicles replace offices, team-building meetings provide yet another place for us to *talk about* work, and just to make everything "homey," we have to endure potluck lunches and birthday celebrations. As so scathingly captured in the sit-com, *The Office,* efforts to make work fun only annoy most of us, especially the introvert.

I talk with many Shadow Dwellers who are mystified by the fact that chatty workers are rarely reprimanded. Sit and gossip and you are fun; close the door (if you have one) and you are antisocial. And we're talking about work here, not a party!

Executives and managers need to consider how introverts—*at least half of their employees*—produce. Employees require energy to produce and, conveniently, introverts come with their own generators. Instead of trying to entertain us, mute the chatter and give us some space. Instead of rewarding the introvert with a party, give her a gift certificate to a restaurant, spa, bookstore, or coffeehouse. Instead of requiring attendance at a staff retreat, give introverted employees their assignments and send them to private cabins. Instead of insisting that introverts attend meetings, give us the option to submit written ideas. Employers are learning that, for many employees, less is more: less discussion, fewer meetings, and less so-called fun.

Another common misunderstanding is that focused workers are grumpy, as if happiness is measured by how much we talk! One introvert complained to me about a coworker: "Every morning she asks me 'What's wrong?' or 'Are you okay?' I hear all the time, 'why don't you smile?' I've been hearing that my whole life!"

> Worst thing about my version of Monday morning: having to interface with extroverted types who want to engage me in what I call "laundromat talk": chatter about the mundane, menial, and morose.
>
> —Don, minister who is drawn to "introspection and spirituality at my pace and in my natural, internal way."

If we are grumpy, perhaps it's because we're tired of being interrupted and interrogated. Short of posting a LEAVE ME ALONE sign on your door (if you *have* a door), how do you minimize the Imposed Work of responding to people? Here are some ideas:

- Identify and communicate your "no talk" zones. If you need time to settle in before talking to anyone, let your coworkers know. If you generally prefer to lunch alone, let your coworkers know. They will be spared any paranoid musings, and you'll be spared the "friendly fire." Consider staggering your work hours so that you arrive earlier or leave later.
- Disarm potential intruders. Make rounds to the people who are likely to intrude on you *before* you get focused. Tell them that you are organizing your day to minimize interruptions. Ask them what they'll need from you, jot it down, and once you've collected these demands, retire to your space.
- If you truly want privacy, be polite *and* discreet. Shadow Dwellers have discreet down, but can actually attract attention by being too abrupt. Silently walking past other employees and slamming your door will probably generate *more* concern and curiosity than offering a simple "Good Morning" as you head toward your office. Though social niceties can serve a protective function, Accessible Introverts can be *too* nice. Stop with "Good Morning" and forgo the "How are you?" Also, tone down the smiles and head nodding. A kind but focused attitude will make it clear you are occupied without ruffling extrovert feathers.
- If you can, designate "office hours"—a time every day when you are available for interruption. Planned interruptions are much easier for an introvert.
- Claim some office space. Review the tips we discussed in Chapter 6, and find out the options offered by your employer. If these don't fit, offer your employer some options. Don't assume you have to sit where you're put.

- When you negotiate a new job or a raise, consider including some peace and quiet in your terms. Be upfront that your strong suit is your ability to work independently and pursue answers without interrupting others. Add that you do best in a setting that allows you to dig in with minimal disruption. The fact that you know your work style and strive to do your best will only impress a potential employer.

- Many work settings utilize the MBTI®, so you may have the opportunity to take the inventory and discuss your work style in this context. You can also express your desire to take the inventory. If you know your "code type," use this as a launching point for discussing your preferred work conditions.

- Though walls are best—and if you've got them, a closed door works wonders—there are other ways of establishing boundaries in a cubicle world. Your facial expression, posture, and way of responding to people can indirectly communicate to people that you are inside yourself and the door is closed.

INTROVERT EXPLOITATION

Another work hazard for introverts is the tendency for supervisors to load work on the people who complain the least. People are often drawn into introvert space because it is less chaotic than extrovert space. Unfortunately, these people bring the chaos in and stress us out. Because we keep our stress inside, extroverts can misread this as, "Sure, I'll take more work!"

Because I give clients so much space *in* their sessions, some of them are surprised to see me stop the sessions on time. These clients sometimes start a new topic after I have noted that we need to end. I am very clear with myself that I cannot be fully available to my clients unless I respect my limits. When clients push it, I stay firm. When the client seems particularly needy, I suggest we meet more frequently—this means paying more, so

> *The worst thing about going to work on a Monday morning is my cheerful co-workers who want to interact and chat the minute I walk in. I once had a boss who had a five-minute rule...as in, no talking in the first five minutes while you get settled, get your coffee, put away your stuff, etc. I think that should be instituted in all workplaces! Maybe she was an introvert too.*
>
> —Karen

the offer is only accepted when the client is really invested, a win-win. Sometimes I tell them frankly that I am no longer attentive once the session time has ended, and that what they say has too much importance for me to listen half-heartedly. I have also sometimes shared a simpler truth: "I like my breaks!"

We cannot ask others to respect our boundaries unless we respect them ourselves. Leave when you say you're going to leave. Ask for the time you need to complete the project—*at your pace.* Introverts can be chronic underestimators, cutting out the thinking time we assume will not be provided. Assume differently. Assume *correctly.* If you are an introvert, assume introversion. Give yourself the time to get clear, live your clarity, and your assumptions will infuse the air. Words won't be necessary. A look will send them running.

CHANGING YOUR MIND

As you assess your work situation, have the courage to, as I tenderly phrase it, "admit what sucks." If you feel like you're back in junior high, surrounded by gossip and social games, move on to adulthood and get a serious job. If you're being flooded with compliments in lieu of pay, take your skills seriously and find a place where value is rewarded with more than words. If you worked your butt off to get to where you are and where you are is disappointing, perhaps it's time to stop doing so much Imposed Work. Or perhaps it's time to move on. A good rule of thumb is that any environment that consistently leaves you feeling bad about who you are is the wrong environment. Have the courage to evaluate your job, to demand more from it, to put it on probation when it is failing you, and to terminate it when necessary. Dream job or no, you have a right to change your mind.

As you admit what sucks, also note those times when your work excites you, when you feel in the zone and positively gleeful about what you're discovering and contributing. Introverts know these experiences because we delight in ideas, and we have the patience and focus to get to the good stuff. Because we work best independently, we can earn ourselves a great deal of freedom. Many of the introverts I corresponded with have found work situations that *work:*

- I'm so comfortable in my current work setting where I have my own office, and sometimes most of the day can go by without me interacting with a co-worker.—Suzanne, paralegal for public defender team
- Most of my sense of accomplishment comes from working with people in individual settings, by listening, advising, encouraging, helping. In the past, some people's personality styles would throw me off track or discourage me from engaging with them to find common ground. I can now meet each day's stress and chaos by applying well established (internalized) reasoning and negotiating tactics.—Phil, health and safety funding specialist
- I am fortunate to have a private office so I can isolate myself and get on task.—Julie, hydrologist
- I like my decorated cubicle world, love where the office is (third floor, away from tribal warfare on the second), love my boss. I love that I can walk down three flights and hit the street, just to stride, to see, to breathe fresh air and feel wind, rain, sunshine on my face.—Doug, editor and producer of online multimedia magazine
- What I love about my work: It's got just the right mix of working alone and working with other people...I like meeting people by working with them and getting to know them that way. It's a lot less tiring to me than being at a party and having to make small talk with people

you're never going to see again. Through work I've made many friends (and acquired a husband).—Ingrid, internal auditor for a large electric utility

- I have a very private cube and a quiet general area, and I do like my immediate group…I love the mental challenge of work, [especially] when I get absorbed.—Karen, corporate real estate finance specialist

IDEA, INC.

Whether you work in a bustling office building or in a wilderness reserve, you were brought there by an idea. Perhaps, like Ingrid, the idea of mastering puzzles and fixing problems led the way. Or, like Doug, you looked for a vehicle for your evolving creative ideas. Like many of us, you might have had an idea about how you could help.

As we get busy with the work, however, it's easy to forget the idea that started it all. Anchoring yourself in your idea is a great way to restore meaning to your work—or to find work that has meaning.

Think back on books, television programs, or movies that inspired you, and read or watch them again. In 1980, the movie *Ordinary People* solidified my idea about becoming a therapist. I watched it again twenty years later and was surprised that its power had not diminished. And there was an added richness: I recognized myself in the story.

As you dig up ideas from your past, you might learn something new about what you were looking for. You might read your own journal entries in a new way or notice a theme running through your sources of inspiration. In contrast to *Ordinary People,* I was also inspired by a more lighthearted source: psychologist Bob Hartley of *The Bob Newhart Show.* As I've revisited the sitcom, I saw my love of acting, comedy, and quirkiness added to the idea of becoming a psychologist.

Another way to recharge your idea is to attend a conference or lecture on the topic. If you left a treasured idea behind when you started working, all the more reason to look into it. If old ideas no longer fit, notice how your thinking and values have evolved. You might even want to create a narrative or timeline of your evolving ideas.

Respect your introversion and your ideas, and the power will come. Richard Florida, in his book, *The Rise of the Creative Class,* proposes that our society is moving toward a "knowledge-driven economy." The Internet doesn't require golf outings and schmoozing; we can connect through ideas—develop a business, teach a course, conduct research—at our own pace and from our own space. Ideas are becoming society's power centers, and introverts are natural generators.

Perhaps we can begin to share ideas in place of "what we do." And our ideas can *become* what we do. Florida's book and others, like *The Opt-Out Revolt* by Lisa A. Mainiero and Sherry E. Sullivan and *Free-Agent Nation* by Daniel H. Pink, note that lifestyles are increasingly built around individuals and ideas rather than groups and organizations.

Ideas are *us.* Introvert power can, if properly managed, efficiently advance every field of human endeavor, from science to business, education to politics. Leaders need only drop the scales from their eyes to produce more, much more, with the people they already employ.

Chapter 14:
The Downside to
Self-Containment

One may have a blazing hearth in one's soul, and yet no one ever comes to sit by it.
—Vincent Van Gogh

Houses have long been seen as symbols of the self. You bring into your house what you value. You decide what comes in and what you take out. You select what to put on the walls and in the rooms. But not only is the house a container; it is also a *structure* with particular features. A house may be vertically oriented, like a city townhouse, or horizontally expansive, like a one-story ranch home. The house may be mobile, or rooted in a deep foundation. Materials range from a stone or brick fortress to the polyester of a yurt.

You probably drew houses as a child, whether spontaneously or for school, and you had a particular way of drawing them. What did they look like? I remember that the windows in my houses always had mullions and curtains—the tieback kind. Were there any special features you always included in your house? If you'd like, draw a house right now. Don't think about it. Just draw a house, and see what you come up with.

If we think of the introvert as a house, he or she may have many windows but few entrances. The home's style is highly personal. There may be, as Van Gogh put it, a "blazing hearth" inside, burning with insight and creativity. The décor may be utilitarian and minimalist—emphasizing key values or practical considerations—or it may be filled with collected treasures. The upper floor might house libraries or laboratories, simmering and bubbling with ideas. When we talk of "what's going on upstairs," we are using the house metaphor.

Though entrances for people are usually closed, and sometimes locked, your house may be open to other life sources. The top floor might have an entrance to worlds beyond—the realms of spirit or fantasy. The ground floor might be the womb of nature, dirt as flooring and living trees as beams. Your home may have a level descending deep into the earth, a place of psychological or historical excavation.

The introvert loves exploring this space, and here finds entertainment and resources for living. While selected people have the code to get in, many others are curious about the home but don't have access. Directions to the house may be complicated and obscure.

THE LONELY HEARTH

So what's wrong with this picture? Our interiors are comfortable, interesting, and protected from intruders. My muse for answering this question is a risky choice: Vincent Van Gogh. He is risky because he was mentally ill—posthumously diagnosed with bipolar disorder and, as we've discussed, introversion is a normal personality dimension. But I remember an important lesson from my graduate training: every mental disorder is only an extreme of the human condition. If you want to understand human vulnerability, study mental illness.

And if you want to know the extreme "poles" of introversion, study Van Gogh. The artist's inner fire lit up his canvases with brilliant color, texture, and feeling. But he longed to share his gifts with a companion, to bring someone in who would not be threatened, but warmed, by his fire.

Van Gogh was an introvert with an amazing interior, an interior that was the best of him but eventually *got* the best of him. It is interesting to note that he found an old house in the south of France, transforming it into what would be known as the Yellow House—the space that would become the seat of his dreams. In a fascinating book, aptly named *The Yellow House,* art critic Martin Gayford describes Van Gogh's color scheme:

> The outside walls were the fresh, almost edible color of butter. The shutters were vivid green, the door inside a soothing blue. There, in and on the house, were the major notes in the color scale—yellow, green, blue, and the rich red of the studio floor.

Gayford, who chronicles Van Gogh's story in astonishing detail, also notes that the primary decorative feature in the house was his collection of paintings, generously adorning the walls of every room. In addition to painting the house, he painted *paintings* of the house and of some of the rooms. The yellow house *was* art.

Like Van Gogh, we want our best to be seen. Most of us have had the experience of creating beauty, whether by cleaning a room, planting a bed of flowers or hanging a painting. Our first impulse is to say, "Come and see! Look what I did!" Though it may be a long time since mom or dad came to see, we still have the need to share—to be seen, acknowledged, appreciated. But it's more than approval we seek; we want to extend the joy. We want someone to help us make it more real, to linger with us in the warmth.

We are wise to be selective about whom we let in. But it is also good to find worthy guests.

A LIMITED VIEW

Van Gogh had taken Paul Gauguin into his imagination long before they shared an actual house. Van Gogh admired

Gauguin: Here was a real poet. Gauguin would be a friend who could appreciate Van Gogh's fire. They would have a studio together and build a sort of monastic community of artists. In the house of Van Gogh's mind, they were aspiring to something great.

As humans, we have the ability to hold relationships and conversations inside, and this capacity helps us work through conflicts, tolerate separations, fall in love, and remember. In fact, imagining a prototype of the person you want in your life can help you find a desirable partner. The stronger your desire, the more likely you will "go for it" and meet someone who matches your criteria.

Van Gogh had a highly developed imagination, and was bold in pursuing the man he was sure would fulfill his vision. He even prepared a room for Gauguin in the yellow house. His vision would become reality.

There was only one problem with Van Gogh's vision: Gauguin. The chosen collaborator was very reluctant to move to the studio, and only gave in after a financial incentive sweetened the deal. Though the collaboration was artistically fruitful, the relationship was a disaster.

What is sad to me is that Van Gogh had a beautiful vision. He was just unable to see enough of what was happening *outside* to realize that Gauguin was not a good match. At the extreme, this unwillingness to modify fantasy becomes a *schizoid* defense. The idea is, "by keeping people inside, in fantasy, I can stay in control and can't be hurt"—though this reasoning is not conscious. Van Gogh did risk a real relationship with the real Gauguin, and *was* hurt—irreparably. After only nine weeks, Gauguin reluctantly shared his plan to leave and the already unstable Van Gogh unraveled. That night, the visionary marked his descent into madness by cutting off his left ear.

I think Van Gogh is such a sympathetic character because we know what it feels like to invest in someone who does not or cannot reciprocate. The vision or *idea* of the relationship can be very powerful, and has a magnetism of its own. These are the visions that seduce lovers and break down defenses.

But, if not checked by reality, even the most beautiful idea can break down and break hearts.

It is easy to forget that our inner representations of people are always limited. And, even when we look out of the house called the Self, we can get the wrong impression through our windows. Let's say a friend walks by with a scowl on her face. Then you go up to your imagination library and tell yourself a story about why she's mad. In your mind, you overhear her saying all kinds of bad things about you. By the time the real friend stops over, you're the one who is mad.

If you had asked her, you might have found out that she had just gotten fired and was deep into her thoughts about it. She didn't even *see* you. Though everyone fills in blanks about other people, introverts are particularly vulnerable to this. Because we limit our interactions, we may miss opportunities for "reality testing," or checking our perceptions with the source.

Beyond the problem of Van Gogh's choice is perhaps a larger question: Was the artist's unwillingness to compromise inseparable from the fire that created such otherworldly beauty? As he prepared and lived in the Yellow House, Van Gogh completed *over two hundred paintings,* including the *Sunflowers* paintings and *The Café Terrace at Night.* Van Gogh's own words suggest that he had some awareness of the price of his passion: "It is better to be high-spirited even though one makes mistakes, than to be narrow-minded and all too prudent."

Though the question I pose can never really be answered, and Van Gogh's illness no doubt made him more vulnerable, the artist's legacy provides valuable insight into the risks of self-contained fantasy. Perhaps the lesson is to be "high-spirited" or high-minded in preparing the house, but more prudent when deciding whom to invite in. Or maybe we'll "go for it," but with eyes wide open, knowing that some mistakes are worth it. Then hopefully, after dusting ourselves off, we'll get up and risk making *more* worthy mistakes. Whatever we do, we can be more conscious. And with the tool of choice, our power will not only be in the vision. We can have our vision and reality too.

SELF-REPROACH

Introverts tend to *internalize* problems. In other words, we place the source of problems *within* and blame ourselves. Though introverts may also *externalize* and see others as the problem, it's more convenient to keep the problem "in house." Internalizers tend to be reliable and responsible, but we can also be very hard on ourselves. And we can be *wrong* about ourselves. Van Gogh would not have been an easy person to live with—when manic, he was prone to verbosity and could become redundant and annoying. He was a slob and a bad cook. But Gauguin wasn't a cup of tea either—he was known to be arrogant, self-absorbed, and grandiose.

With all of Gauguin's complaints about Van Gogh, the latter artist seemed blind to his colleague's limitations. Even as Gauguin was walking out the door, Van Gogh felt he was losing someone he desperately needed. And Van Gogh blamed himself.

As an introvert, you can be your own best friend or your worst enemy. The good news is we generally like our own company, a quality that extroverts often envy. We find comfort in solitude and know how to soothe ourselves. Even our willingness to look at ourselves critically is often helpful.

But, we can go too far. We can hoard responsibility and overlook the role others play. We can kick ourselves when we're down. How many times have you felt lousy about something, only to get mad at yourself for feeling lousy?

As a therapist, I see this tendency in extroverts as well as introverts, but extroverts are more likely to seek out reassurance from others. And introverts are more likely to use internalization as a convenience: if we keep things in-house, we don't have to involve extroverts.

It is helpful for introverts to remember that we can keep things inside and still recognize what's outside. An introvert playing the Van Gogh role in a relationship can choose to face facts and, rather than turning on himself, can just let the other person go—preferably *before* that person moves in. Here are other ways to stay on your own side:

- First, notice how you talk to yourself. It can be very helpful to write down an inner conversation, especially one that includes a stream of judgment and criticism. You can also use feelings as a cue: if you are feeling "beat up"—depressed mood, low energy—see if you are beating yourself up. What are you telling yourself?

- Stop the destructive conversation, and "call out" the hurtful message. When I catch myself, I might just say, "That's mean!" and start over, addressing myself more kindly. In an approach called *narrative therapy,* problems are purposely externalized to allow for these confrontations. For example, if it's Guilt that goes after you, you talk back to Guilt. If it's Fear, you'll give Fear a piece of your mind. I worked with a musician who learned to tell Pressure to back off so he could enjoy his performances.

- When we criticize ourselves, we often disown aspects of ourselves that we value. Try changing your criticism into an affirmative statement. For example, "I'm too sensitive" is critical, but "I'm sensitive" is neutral. You are stating and accepting the truth as you see it. Where "too sensitive" imposes an external criterion, "sensitive" stands alone. You are in the center.

- Practice being kind to yourself. Lovingly observe your way of being in the world. See the wisdom in your pace, your manner, and your choices—even the bad choices. It's fine to want to change some things, but change is easier from a position of acceptance. Treat yourself with respect.

- Give others credit for their part in problems. You don't have to confront everyone who makes a mistake, but it helps to be clear about the location of the problem. Sometimes we just need to let the other person wrestle with it.

STALE AIR

Introverts are not afraid of being alone, because we know that solitude is generative. We prefer to take problems and work on them in isolation. We're not big on study groups or committees. And most of us do very well on our own. But, sometimes, staying closed off can become a burden and deprive us of fresh perspectives. Sometimes we need to unload, shake out the rugs, and let in some air.

If you pay attention, you can probably tell when the air inside is getting stale. You feel mentally stuck, bored with your own thinking, or overwhelmed by the intensity within. You're not having any fun. Ironically, these may be the very times you feel immobilized. The introvert preference for "figuring it out" keeps you locked inside. Writers know this experience: we torture over a sentence, writing and rewriting. Then, when we finally have the courage to leave the scene of the bad sentence and go for a walk, the right words pop into our minds.

Sometimes a Breath Retreat does the trick, but other times we need the fresh perspective of a new mind, a sounding board. Sometimes it's a relief to let someone else do the thinking as you rest your mind. And sometimes, talking *does* help—that is, if the other person knows how to listen. As you talk it through, your ideas become more tangible—as if projected onto a virtual reality screen, where you can move them around, sort them out and get to the "ah-ha!"

A related pitfall for introverts is "information deprivation." We can waste a lot of time going through mental contortions, searching for an answer when a quick question might be all that is needed. Because this option does not readily come to mind, the beauty of asking for help can be a startling revelation to the introvert. Though the Internet is a great resource, we can get stuck in our cyberspace searches as well. Sometimes there is no substitute for a live contact.

So how do we know when it's time to reach out? And when it's time, how do we leave that nice, cozy interior of solitude?

Try these strategies:

- Observe yourself. Just notice when solitude feels generative and when it feels confining. Do you want to be here, or are you just stuck in your thoughts? At the end of your day, note what worked and what didn't. Remember to be a kind observer.
- Do you actually need *more* solitude? Sometimes, even when we're alone, our surroundings—the phone, email messages, and clutter—distract us. If this is the case, you may need a retreat rather than a person. Close your mailbox, step away from the computer. It's hard, I know. Just. Walk. Away. Practice leaving the demands behind, even for five minutes. Get air.
- Other times, you may experience "introvert overload" and become either overwhelmed or bored with your own inner process. Maybe your head is cluttered because you have taken too much in and thrown too little out. Or, alternatively, your inner space has gotten a bit drab and could use some fresh furnishings. These are times when human contact helps. Share what you've got and bring in some new ideas.
- As we've discussed, sometimes we take in concerns that really belong to someone else. Sort out what is yours and what isn't. Clean your house: if it isn't yours, delegate it, throw it out of your mind, or give it back. Because introverts seem to have a lot of room, we can become storage facilities for the problems of others. You don't have to accept every delivery that arrives at your door.
- Sometimes it's refreshing to have someone else talk, to have a distraction from our own problems. If you're bored with your own company, ask somebody in your world to tell you what's new. Learn about something entirely new.
- Sleep on it. Anecdotal and experimental evidence support the wisdom of letting ideas simmer overnight. People who sleep on it seem to do better than those who toil away. If you're stuck, try calling it a night.

LOSS OF COMMUNITY

Because introverts often keep "one foot out" of the group, we can lose a sense of belonging—a sense that we are part of something. Like Van Gogh, you may have an idea of the kind of community you crave but have a hard time finding it. When I moved to West Virginia, I envisioned myself as part of a bohemian artists' community. As a wife and mother of school-aged boys, this may have seemed like a stretch—and it *was*. I needed to stretch beyond my immediate surroundings to find "my people." I was overly eager. I made mistakes and got hurt. But, ultimately I found my community by pursuing what I loved: writing, acting, art, coffeehouses. And my community evolves as I evolve.

For introverts, the best associations start with *ideas*. If you don't feel a part of your neighborhood association or the happy hour regulars after work, don't force it. The community that surrounds you may not be *your* community. Give yourself the gift of an outside world that represents you. Volunteer for a cause you care about. Post an online profile and find other people who love Elvis, quantum physics, and tennis. Audition for a play or audit a college course. Attend a workshop or a conference on something that fascinates you. Do what you love a little more publicly, and your people will come.

We like communities that are easy, where people welcome us without binding us. However, it is not always necessary to meet to feel the comfort of a community. We establish remote associations when we read, pray, or listen to music. And, as an introvert, you are automatically part of a very large community, though we aren't likely to set up any meetings.

As with Van Gogh, when your ideas hit the world, the plot thickens. You encounter disappointment and frustration— every good story has these elements. As long as you stay on your own side and keep your eyes open, learning as you go, the downside won't keep you down.

Chapter 15:
Showing Up for
Relationships

Oh, the comfort—the inexpressible comfort of feeling safe with a person—having neither to weigh thoughts nor measure words, but pouring them all right out.

—Dinah Craik

For introverts, relationships create a paradox. We crave safe, comfortable, intimate, small-talk-free connections. But we also want ample time to ourselves, space of our own, and quiet. Some of us want a relationship at the center of our lives, and some of us want solitude at the center. Many of us want both.

How do we work this paradox? How do we maintain relationships—*close* relationships—and still have the alone time that sustains us? What happens if we marry? And what if we want kids?

We are culturally conditioned to want and seek out the relationship side of the paradox, but we get very little validation for the "alone time" part. I am married, very happily, and we have two boys that I couldn't wait to conceive and bring into our world. I am one of ten children, though, and I needed therapy to help me accept my scandalous wish to stop having children at two. I knew that I would shortchange the two we had if we added more. I was certain I would shortchange myself; I had reached my interpersonal maximum. Thankfully, I had the space of my analysis to sort this out and to contend with all my training to believe "the more the better." I have never looked back.

But if it was scandalous for me to stop at two, what about the many introverts who prefer not to have kids? What about those who prefer to stay single? In "America the extroverted," relationships are good, and even if they are very bad, they are better than no relationship. Introverts don't think this way. Many of us want and have great relationships, but we generally prefer "no relationship" to a bad one. Quality matters. We conserve our relationship resources, because we know they are limited. We probably see ourselves as having *less* to offer a relationship than we actually do; extroverts generally think they have more to offer. This is not because extroverts are arrogant, but because America is about quantity, and extroverts revel in quantity.

> Q: How do you prefer to interact with people?
> A: Short periods at a time, intense or not.
>
> —J. C., artist

But when an introvert is self-aware enough to say "no" to a relationship that he is not willing to invest in, we assume he is afraid or selfish. When a woman says "no" to having babies, we assume she is selfish and "missing something." In these assumptions, we neglect what is often missing for the socially preoccupied extrovert: the nourishment of the inner life.

While in my analysis, I had a series of dreams about babies. The repeating theme was: I had the baby, and then would forget her. Depending on the dream, I might have left her at the hospital or in her crib, or forgotten to feed her. I would suddenly remember my responsibility, then be horrified that I had forgotten. The other running theme in the dreams was that the baby was precocious: she would talk or walk almost immediately; she learned how to manage. I still feel the heartbreak of recognizing this baby who was forced to grow up without nourishment.

That baby, of course, was the neglected part of me: my introversion. Caring for the part of you that is not ready to talk, that part that is waiting for you to slow down and notice, *is* your responsibility. And we also have a responsibility to the people we choose to have in our lives. How do we attend to the life inside *and* our loved ones outside?

THE PROBLEM OF FAMILY

In America, the term "family values" has become a political and social rallying point. We don't really know what it means, but we know it's good—something we should have. Any spin on this theme tends to get swallowed without question: "Family comes first," "Family is the bedrock of society," blah, blah, blah.

Introverts are often very close to family members. We like the familiarity, the shared history, the opportunity to bypass small talk. But the "family comes first" idea is often foreign to introverts. We are wired to start inside: many of us couldn't start outside if we wanted to. We are centered inside, and we like it that way.

Family was at the center of my childhood home, and I knew that I was not a part of that center. I was loved—that wasn't it. I just didn't function that way. The physical structure of our home mirrored this reality. The living room was the "family room." This room was the gathering place, the center. I did not live in the living room. And I still don't. My husband, the extrovert, lives in the living room. I do more of my living in *my* room and *visit* the living room, as I did in my childhood home. The exception to this is when I have the house to myself: then the entire house is "my room." These days are sweet.

My impulse right now, from my cultural programming, is to explain how much I love my boys and my husband, but I really don't want to do that. I don't talk a whole lot about my family, because I don't talk a whole lot about *people*. When I'm with them, I'm really with them, but I don't tell everyone what they're doing, and I won't suffer "empty nest syndrome."

My center will not be torn when my boys go off to college. I will miss them, but my relationship is less dependent on proximity. I hold them inside wherever they are.

It's different for my husband, the extrovert. He will be torn, and he knows it. His *interactions* with the boys, and with me, are at his center. He holds them inside too, but that's not his center. Let me illustrate with a conversation we had recently. I'll use "E" for him, the extrovert, and "I" for me:

> E: At dinner, you look like you can't wait to leave.
> I: That's true; sitting at dinner is hard for me.
> E: But it's dinner! The family meal. The time we are together! How could anything be more important?
> I: It's not my thing.
> E: It's the family meal. It's *the* thing!
> I: Yes, for you it is. But who says it has to be *the* thing? I like to respond to the kids when they're hungry. I'd just as soon feed them individually. I also prefer talking with them, and with you, individually. Is that not as valid?

We had been married twenty-four years, and this was the first time I said these words out loud—in the affirmative rather than in an apology. My husband, a passionate trial attorney, respected my argument. I actually like the fact that he rallies us for dinner, and I think there is a place for family rituals. But I don't share his *desire,* and it is freeing to say so. My individualized approach to meals has also benefited our boys: they only eat when they're hungry and eat only as much as they want. But *that* un-American concept is for another book.

INTROVERSION AND INTIMACY

Even though introverts are good at sustaining relationships internally, we need to inform and update our inside versions of loved ones. If we don't update, we might hold onto a fantasy, as Van Gogh did, or an earlier version of a person—something that happens in many marriages. In order to update, we need contact. When an introvert cares about someone, she also *wants* contact, not so much to keep up with the events of the other person's life, but to keep up with what's *inside:* the evolution of ideas, values, thoughts, and feelings.

When we live with someone, we can more easily move in and out of contact without too much planning. With a friend, keeping up is more of a challenge. I have two best friends, and I love being with each of them. Two of my sisters are also my intimate friends. I want time with each of these loved ones, but sometimes that desire is more theoretical than practical. Because, when I'm feeling low, I'm more likely to seek out solitude instead of a friend. When I'm tired, I recharge through solitary activity. When I want to see a movie, I prefer to go alone.

Yet, the older I get, the more I value my friends, and by some miracle, I am a good friend to them. Here are the strategies behind the miracle:

- Schedule a standing date. This works great with a partner, child, or friend. Cindy and I have a standing lunch—a *long* lunch—every Wednesday. If one of us can't make it, we just cancel, but otherwise there is no need to set anything up. The regular time becomes a touchstone. We have moved it to after work at times when lunch isn't good, but we can count on seeing each other regularly. When I feel too much distance in any of my key relationships, I set up a date. This has worked well with my sons. I enjoy, as Anne Morrow Lindbergh wrote about in *Gifts from the Sea,* the "across the table" time with just one other person. Though I may be efficient at the family table, I linger at the table for two.
- Get away together. My husband and I try to match up short work excursions—he goes to court, I write. The drive time gives us leisurely time to talk, away from the distractions of family life, and we sometimes work in an overnight stay. I also have enjoyed retreating with one or two introverted friends: a mini monastic experience—

though sometimes with tequila. We stay in a cabin in a natural setting and enjoy quiet time, some solitary, some shared, and very, very low-key. The ample space of the retreat allows us to move past the layers of daily concerns to the stuff we really care about.

- Email your updates. It often fits better into the flow of my day to send an email update to a friend than to call. Like many introverts, I am freer with my fingers than with my mouth anyway, so they get the real deal more quickly. When I vent via email, I show a crude side of myself that few people see.

- Get together for solitary activity. Beth and I do this: we meet at a coffeehouse to write or read, and intersperse conversation into the flow. I find this "alone together" time very soothing, and try to foster this atmosphere in our home. I think of Fred Pine, the child development theorist, who wrote about the importance of "quiet pleasure," or "low-keyed pleasure in nonthreatening doses" to the development of healthy children.

Ironically, introverts often crave *more* time with the key people in their lives. We need this time to allow the inner life of both self and other to emerge without force. Lindbergh captures this organic quality in her description of the "pure relationship":

The pure relationship, how beautiful it is! How easily it is damaged, or weighed down with irrelevancies—not even irrelevancies, just life itself, the accumulations of life and of time. For the first part of every relationship is pure, whether it be with friend or lover, husband or child. It is pure, simple, and unencumbered. It is like the artist's vision before he has to discipline it into form.

LOVING OUR EXTROVERTS

The scenarios I have been describing flow quite easily with another introvert. When the extrovert enters, as much as we love him or her, things get a bit more complicated—or a *lot* more complicated, depending on how much extroversion we are talking about.

Before we get to the "why can't we all be friends" part, I've gathered some complaints we, the introverts, need to get off our chests. So, here it is: The ***Introvert Power*** "Extroverts at their Most Annoying" Top 10 list:

10. When everything has to be a PARTY!
 9. When E will not accept that you really want to *leave* the party.
 8. When E calls too often, talks too much, and says too little.
 7. When "E The Intruder" enters your space, uninvited, and handles your stuff.
 6. When you go out together and E talks to the stranger sitting beside you.
 5. When an E you don't know asks, "Are you okay?" just because you're quiet.
 4. When E calls to respond to the email you sent because you didn't want to talk.
 3. When E brings someone along to your "one on one"— as a *surprise.*
 2. When E takes cell phone calls during your time alone.
 1. When E assumes every silence is an invitation to TALK.
 1. When E talks at length without a single pause.
 1. When the above behavior requires you to interrupt in order to speak.
 1. When you finally get to speak, and your words remind E of something else to share.
 1. When E is oblivious to all attempts to end the conversation, including "goodbye" and walking away.

Okay, we had a few more than ten, and a few competitors for number one. But before my extroverted sisters and friends start calling me with complaints (when I'd really prefer they send an email), I will say that the socially oblivious extroverts do not represent the whole. As with introverts, social skills are independent of extroversion: some are skilled, some are not. The skilled ones know how to listen. But in contrast to socially unskilled introverts, who keep to themselves, socially unskilled extroverts insist on *socializing*.

Introvert conversations are like jazz, where each player gets to solo for a nice stretch before the other player comes in and does his solo. And like jazz, once we get going, we can play all night. Extrovert conversations are more like tennis matches, where thoughts are batted back and forth, and players need to be ready to respond. Introverts get winded pretty quickly.

But, as challenging as our extroverts may be, they provide a balance we crave. The introverts I polled described extroverts as "upbeat" and able to "keep things light" and "cheer you up." Some admired the ability of extroverts to "work a room" without self-consciousness. Even when I am annoyed with my little sister for talking to everyone in close proximity, I admire how much she loves *people*. She is a best friend to the world, and people respond to her with as much love as she radiates. I have especially appreciated this quality in her when she is around my friends.

Having an extroverted friend or partner can be an advantage. He can clear a path through the social jungle, answer phone calls, and haggle with the salesperson. He can also keep the introvert informed of the social world on a "want to know" basis (though we don't want to know all that much). Having an extrovert attend to externals frees the introvert to indulge in her preference.

> *It takes an extrovert to bring out my upbeat side. If it were up to me, everyone would probably just sit around talking about mysteries of the universe.*
>
> —Solveig, who appreciates an occasional retreat from her depth

When I consulted with my extroverts, they said they appreciate introverts because we listen well and don't compete for attention. Just as the extroverted host frees an introvert to keep a low profile, we give extroverts room to talk and enjoy the spotlight.

The problem is, introverts don't always enjoy listening, and extroverts don't always enjoy greeting the guests. In an introvert-extrovert relationship, the introvert often sees the extrovert as selfish in conversations—interrupting or too easily responding with her own comments. The extrovert sees the introvert's need for alone time as selfish.

If we are to work through our differences, both sides need to throw down the selfish accusation, acknowledge that we are different, and communicate. When we accept and *respect* our differences, the rest is not that hard. What this means, on both sides, is admitting the limitations of our understanding and becoming more *curious* about each other. If all extroverts can say about us is that we're weird, they don't know us. And if all we can say about extroverts is that they're shallow, we don't know them. The wonderful thing about loving an extrovert is that there is *so much to learn* about each other—there's little room for boredom. Jung said that we choose partners in order to expand who we are. After almost three decades of knowing each other, my husband and I keep discovering new dimensions of each other. He recently shared a painful dimension of life with an introvert:

> The way you relish being away from me…it's painful—*literally*. You withdraw an energy source. I gather life from being around other people. When you "drift away," I lose energy. I lose *life*. It's as if I'm watching a movie and somebody turns the power off. I'm sitting there, wondering why the movie stopped.

This was a revelation to me, because my husband seems to be so independent. He does *not* always want to talk, and we both have our own interests and friends. But I *have* sensed his annoyance when I drift away, and we've even talked about it before. But this time, he showed me what *he* experiences, and that made all the difference. When an extroverted friend begs you to stay at a party, she may not get how hard it is for you to stay, but perhaps you don't get how hard it is for her to see you leave.

The irony of my husband's disclosure is that *I* have felt a similar frustration with introverts from time to time. I know what it feels like to lose a reclusive friend who "drops off the face of the Earth" indefinitely to sort something out, unable or unwilling to give me any read on what was going on. It sucks.

My husband—I love this about him—did not ask me to stick around more, but just asked that I provide "more loving separations." For the friend at the party, this might be: "I know you're having a lot of fun and it doesn't feel good for me to cut out, but I'm really shot." This simple act acknowledges the impact of the introvert vanishing act. It ultimately helps us too, because when our extroverts are reassured, we can relax. I feel my husband's frustration when he expects me back in a minute and I'm gone for a half hour. Ironically, keeping him apprised frees me up.

A simple adjustment—that is often what it comes down to. Here are some other adjustments you might try:

- Attend to your flock first. What introverts don't always realize is that withholding our attention can set us up for intrusion. Child-development expert T. Berry Brazelton advises parents just getting home from work to give ten minutes of undivided attention to their children right away. Assured of the parents' presence, the children soon get bored and go back to their activities. Introverted parents can then relish some guilt-free solitude, without the children tugging at them, demanding attention. This works with spouses and coworkers too.

- When you go to lunch with an extrovert who gets interrupted by her cell phone, try using the disruption as a slice of solitude within the conversation. Bring something you're reading or a journal to write in, or just sit back and observe the scene around you. Let the extrovert's detachment work in your favor, creating that "alone together" feeling.

- As an experiment and as an act of love, try sticking it out with an extrovert, whether the "it" is a party or a group conversation. When I have done this, I notice something shifting for me. I submit, lose my concern about time, and realize that it won't kill me. I expect very little, and there's something liberating in that. I think the same thing happens when extroverts submit to solitude: they move past the restlessness, realize it won't kill them, and enjoy giving in to the experience.

RELATIONSHIP ASSESSMENT

In Chapter 13, we looked at the difference between Natural Work and Imposed Work. This is a useful distinction to make as we assess relationships as well. The relationships that we *naturally* work to improve are the ones that keep getting better—and easier. The ones that we have to push ourselves to attend to, either because the other person is neglectful or because we're not that interested—or *both*—are the ones that keep getting harder.

Introvert-introvert relationships generate less conflict, are more comfortable, and flow more easily. Less time is spent *forging* the relationship, so more time can be spent *expressing* the relationship. But because there is no extrovert in the mix, the functions of initiating and maintaining outside contacts are either shared by the couple or picked up by the more extroverted partner. There is less of a "one out front, one behind the scenes" arrangement. Introvert-extrovert relationships are more prone to conflict and require more communication and self-awareness. They can also promote more growth.

However, either combination may be Natural Work for an introvert. The key is not the combination of personality types, but the mutual desire to be together. When you're in the relationship out of some sense of obligation, or for any agenda other than desire, even the easiest combination will be work— the kind we *avoid*.

One of the gifts of introversion is that we have to be discriminating about our relationships. We know we only have so much energy for reaching out; if we're going to invest, we want it to be good. When your assessment is done and you hit on a winner, just don't forget to show up and reap the rewards.

Part IV:
Outing the Introvert

Chapter 16:
From Apology to
Acceptance—and
Beyond

I said to myself, "I have things in my head that are not like what anyone has taught me"…
I decided to start anew—to strip away what I had been taught—to accept as true my own thinking.
—Georgia O'Keefe

I remember first reading O'Keefe's words and considering her radical choice. How would my life be different if I *accepted as true* my own thinking? The idea was so simple, yet incredibly liberating. "Accepting as true" would mean no more reaching, defending or explaining—no more contorted attempts to line myself up with the world. If I were to accept my thinking, life would be straightforward. I'd free up a lot of energy. As O'Keefe noted, acceptance requires stripping away, unlearning, cleaning out the additives we heap on top of our thinking.

If we are to reclaim our power as introverts, we would do well to follow O'Keefe's lead. We have talked about unlearning old assumptions and stripping away the clutter of our extroverted culture. In this chapter, you will unlearn the habit of apologizing for introversion, and learn to *accept as true* what you really think.

Try accepting as true the thought, "the party will not be fun." Imagine looking curiously at the extrovert who talks about how fun the party will be. Consider staying rooted in your own thinking while others flail about.

Feels good, doesn't it? The shift from apology to acceptance, while monumental, does not require a speech or even a witty retort. In most cases, words are not necessary. In fact, we more often use words to *defend* our thinking, which usually implies that the thinking *needs something else*—support, justification, apology.

APOLOGIES, EXPLANATIONS, AND EXCUSES

How often do you apologize, explain, or make excuses for being introverted? If you were to track these behaviors for a day or two you may be surprised. Introverts often pull out all three methods—the apology, explanation, *and* excuse—in declining an invitation:

> E: Why don't you come along after work? A bunch of us are going out for martinis.
>
> I: (feeling caught) Oh…shoot! I've gotta…I promised Julie I'd pick her up, and the kids have stuff…Darn, I'll have to catch you next time. I'm really sorry. It sounds like fun.
>
> E: You could invite Julie along.
>
> I: Yeah, thing is, I know she was working late and she just wanted to keep it low key. But thanks for suggesting it! You guys have fun!
>
> E: Well, if you're sure.
>
> I: Yeah, but thanks again. Drink an extra one for me! I'll have to catch you next time!

For some of you, this conversation probably seems over-the-top. Others of you will wonder if I've been recording you. It is a quirk of human nature to make up the more elaborate excuses for the things we want to do the least.

But we often don't stop at making excuses. We also feign enthusiasm and regret—again, it seems, in proportion to how little we want to go. Let's try this conversation the O'Keefe way:

> E: Why don't you come along after work? A bunch of
> us are going out for martinis.
> I: (feeling caught) Hmm…I don't think so, but thanks!

That's it! In this scenario, the introvert declined without explanation or apology, while also thanking the extrovert for the invitation. Let's say the extrovert pushes it:

> E: But it's really fun! They have twenty-four different
> kinds of martinis!
> I: [You could stay silent, indicating that your choice
> stands, or clarify] Wow. Yeah, it's just not what I
> want to do. Sounds like you'll have fun, though.
> E: Yeah, I always have a good time when I go there.

What's nice about this conversation—and the introvert *is* being nice—is that the introvert allows the extrovert her reality ("it's really fun!") without making it *his* reality ("not really what I want to do"). The introvert gets to keep her reality without asking the extrovert to relinquish hers.

As a Minnesota native, I believe in nice. But I don't believe in misrepresenting who I am, even though I have done so through my apologies. We misrepresent ourselves when we feign disappointment—*when we really feel thrilled*—that we cannot attend something. We don't *mean* to lie, but it just comes out! Does this sound familiar? Someone asks you to go to a social event, and you hear yourself saying, "Oh, I already have other plans. I'm really disappointed. Maybe next time!"

Then you realize that you have just asked to be invited to the next event.

I caught myself doing this when I was invited to a meeting in our neighborhood. A part of me was standing back and watching me lying through my teeth about how I really wanted to make it next time. The observing me was thinking, "What the hell are you talking about? You have no interest in joining that club!"

But that's how programming works: society's assumptions sink in, and we don't even know it until we hear ourselves restating those assumptions—automatically, without thought. We change by becoming aware. We become aware by observing: watching our own conversations, noticing the lies, seeing the truth. And once we get clear about the truth, we can try something radically different: honesty.

> Never apologize for showing feeling. When you do so, you apologize for the truth.
>
> —Benjamin Disreali

Responding honestly *on the spot* is not easy for introverts, but doing so not only feels better but also makes things easier for us in the long run. Excuses only get us out of things *temporarily* and guarantee that the next invitation is just around the corner.

THE PLACE FOR APOLOGY

For all its problems, "I'm sorry" can be a lovely sentiment, even when the problem is not ours or not our fault. We apologize to show respect for another person's feelings. We also apologize in service of social convention. You say, "I'm sorry" when someone loses a loved one through death. You are not taking responsibility for the death. You say you are sorry because the other person is hurting, and because *that's what you say.*

As we discussed in Chapter 5, the social conventions of Japan require a lot of apologies. The Japanese are loathe to bother anyone, and introverts share this value. We don't like bothering others because we don't like being bothered—the Golden Rule in practice. Deference is not such a bad quality:

it communicates a respect for the importance of another person, her space and her privacy. Where deference is a social convention, you will find a more introverted society.

In America, deference is a very unpopular notion. Why would you put yourself "one down" when the whole point is to move up? Why would you back off when you're supposed to get ahead?

These are loaded questions because they assume extroversion. In Introvertia, we take turns stepping back. We see the beauty in the lower position and wisdom in waiting. In this light, the apology question becomes trickier. Do we really want to relinquish the social graces of the Accessible Introvert, or the "out of the way" position of the Shadow Dweller? Do we really want to be more assertive—more *extroverted?*

But being polite protects boundaries, and in this way *serves* introversion. I recall the culture shock of moving to urban New Jersey after living in Minnesota, Colorado, and Nevada. In this brave new world of traffic circles and "jughandles" and fast-paced speech, I noticed something different about sidewalk behavior. Here, when I encountered someone in my path, he didn't move over—*at all.* I would automatically move aside, and was accustomed to the other person doing the same. In fact, I was so accustomed to this mutual accommodation that I hadn't thought about it. Now, I was the only one accommodating. Welcome to life as an introvert.

Ironically, introverts assert introversion by *demonstrating* a more respectful way of interacting. We listen, because we value listening and want others to listen to us as well. We try not to get in other peoples' way, because we don't like being interrupted. We follow the writer's dictum: "show, don't tell." But there's a problem here. *Extroverts don't get it.* Other introverts may not get it either, because Americans are programmed to ignore the subtle. If you say, "I'm sorry" about not participating, others easily translate that as a bow to extroversion: "I'm sorry I can't be a better extrovert." In Japan, both participants bow; in

America, if you bow, you are the only one bending over—a very vulnerable position.

We don't live in Introvertia, but this is not Extrovertia either, as we have been taught to believe. We live in the middle, and I think there is a middle way: a way of addressing the world that is neither rude and aggressive nor harmful to ourselves.

We know that "sorry" is intended to show regard for the *other* person's feelings, rather than to apologize for *our* feelings. But in our diverse society, and especially when communicating with extroverts, it helps to be more deliberate about what the apology is for. You might say:

> I see that you really want me to come. I like that part, and I'm sorry to disappoint you. But what I really want is some time to myself.

This way, you not only show respect for the other person, but you get to be part of the equation.

You can also dispense with the apology and just be polite. Try "No, thank you. I'm looking forward to an evening at home." This is polite, but more accurate than "I'm sorry, but I really need to stay home tonight." In the case of my neighborhood meeting, I could have simply said, "I appreciate that you took the time to include me, but I don't want to add anything to my schedule right now."

INTROVERT INTEGRITY

I used the word "want" in the above example, because this word changes everything. To express want is to *own* the desire, to stand in your own reality. The easier alternative is the language of impairment: "I can't come because I'm run down, overworked, under the gun, tired, sick, or not up to it." The underlying message is, "I cannot attend because I am impaired," rather than the more honest and self-respecting response: "I choose to not attend because I prefer the other option."

By coming off as impaired extroverts, we not only diminish ourselves, but we perpetuate the extroversion assumption. Over and over, we send out messages: "Gosh, I really wish I could, but I've got all this stuff and I'm tired and I just can't do it, but I'm so sorry because it sounds so much better than what I have in mind and of course going out with people is the better choice and being by myself is pathetic and weak and I'm going to spend the evening regretting that I didn't come and for being such a loser."

Communicating the *preference* for introversion requires practice. Start by noticing your internal and external conversations. As you catch yourself in a lie, stop, think, and try something else. Give yourself lots of room to mess up. Rehearse with your partner or a trusted friend. Try out phrases like, "I like to keep my evenings open," "I'm on a writing high and prefer not to be disturbed," or "I prefer small group gatherings."

We want to create a world that is more respectful *and* we want and deserve respect. We cannot afford to wait for extroverts to get it. Introverts have the advantage of an inward perspective, and this is where we can start. How much respect do *you* give your introverted preferences?

One of my introvert passions is writing. Although I have made space in my life for writing, and I am now fortunate enough to get paid to write, I still catch myself making statements like, "I can't [insert extroverted activity]; I *have to* write." At least this is true: I am often on deadline, and publishers expect me to produce. And "having to write" is a great excuse for getting out of things. I can use it any time, because there is always something to write.

The lie here is subtler, but perhaps even more damaging to my integrity. While there are times I "have" to write, more than not, this is what I *want* to be doing. For me, apologizing for writing is like apologizing for time with a lover: "Sorry, I *have* to be with my true love." The content of what I am saying is true, but the implication is a betrayal of myself and a devaluation of what I love.

> *I cannot find language of sufficient energy to convey my sense of the sacredness of private integrity.*
>
> —Ralph Waldo Emerson

Introvert integrity means *going the distance* for what we love: moving from apology to acceptance,. from acceptance to acknowledgement, and from acknowledgment to activism. And just as distance running requires training, we build introvert integrity through practice. We give ourselves regular sessions of solitude. We find friends who listen. We exercise the right to talk less and think more. We allow others to be uncomfortable, disappointed, and different. We practice trusting our own thinking, even when the thoughts "are not like what anyone has taught" us.

When you can say with a smile, "Yes, I'm not an Extrovert," people will want to know what you're up to. They'll wonder what they are missing out on by being so social. And, if they are wise, they'll back off, shut up and wait. Maybe they'll even apologize.

Chapter 17: Celebrating Introversion

[The Introvert] is...in good physical, emotional, and spiritual health...You will find her outside sitting on a large rock looking out over the water or inside looking out the window with a pensive appearance, sometimes reading... Yes, I like this person very much. She is me.

—Donna

Alienated? No. I feel very human; I think I'm more connected than most people.

—Ben

I enjoy horseback riding, reading, hiking, flower gardening...I like that I am not afraid to be alone. I am not afraid of being with myself. I can find lots of things to do if faced with time alone.

—Julie

I feel comfortable with my place in the universe. I'm at peace with my spirituality and humanity. I like my stubbornness. That tenacity is what allows me to stick with things until I'm done. I seldom look back and say, "I wish I'd tried harder."

—Dave

The person whose company I enjoy more than anyone's is my own.

—Margit

Introverts are alive and very well. In the midst of assaults from an extroverted society, pathologizing assumptions, lies, and pressures to conform, we are here—in larger numbers than extroverts! And the same quality that gets attacked, our inward focus, is what keeps us strong.

To some degree, introverts will always be outside of society, and this is not only the key to our health, but to the health of society. We bring something "not of this world" to the world. We have access to a wealth that is not dependent on the gross national product—or subject to the national debt. We reflect while others move ahead. We invent while others rely on what is established. We seek while others produce. We create while others consume. We stay rooted while others waver.

Introverts carry the *yin* function of life. Though personality tests describe introversion in a superficial (westernized) way, the ancient concept of *yin* tells us much more. *Yin* is dark, cool, and receptive, oriented to the moon and the earth. Time to turn out the lights and celebrate the introvert!

LIFE IN THE DARK

In Western society, "dark" has become synonymous with evil. We are taught to distrust what we cannot see. But darkness is also where dreams are made, where babies are formed, and where insights are discovered. The moon symbolizes the genius of introversion: the ability to illuminate this other side of life—the inner life.

Darkness also represents the mysterious beauty of introversion. We are not completely knowable, and this is a key to our attractiveness. Where extroverts air their thoughts as they come, we keep ideas inside as we work them out. The ability to withhold gives us credibility: we are less likely to blurt out statements we can't support. In the 1980s, a commercial for the investment firm E. F. Hutton became a popular mantra: *"When E. F. Hutton talks, people listen."* I recall a boss of mine telling me, "When Laurie Helgoe talks, people listen." This was because I was often silent during team meetings, but when I spoke, everyone paid attention. And I had instant power.

Introverts don't need to get every-thing out into the light. We focus better in the dark. Rather than putting all our cards on the table, we can wait until the time is right, until ideas are fully formed, and until people are ready to hear. I could waste a great deal of energy *giving* my perspective to a client, but if I wait until she asks for it—if I *respond*—my energy is matched by her interest, and she hears me. The squeaky wheel may get the grease, but people don't like to listen to it.

> [I have] a pronounced dark side (not evil, though) that is my "zone of refuge."
>
> —Phil

Dark is also associated with *depression*, something that is as misunderstood as introversion. Clinical depression is an illness, but dark moods are part of life. In Western society, we keep coming up with new strategies for eliminating the dark. In the '50s, we had "the power of positive thinking"; in the '80s, "Feeling Good"…through positive thinking; and, in 2007, "The Secret" of…well, positive thinking. Like Icarus, we convince ourselves that we can merge with the sun without getting burned.

There is a lot to be said for positive thinking, and an exclusive focus on the negative can be destructive. But denial of the negative is just as dangerous. Extroverts describe themselves as happier than introverts; as we discussed in Chapter 7, "pleas-antness" is a priority for extroverts. Extroverts like the light. Earlier, we challenged the assumption that "parties are fun." But there's an assumption within this assumption: *fun is the ultimate goal.*

Here is the problem with evaluating someone else's reality with an assumption that is not shared. Extroverts want us to have fun, because they assume we want what they want. And *sometimes* we do. But "fun" itself is a "bright" word, the kind of word that comes with flashing lights and an exclamation point! One of Merriam-Webster's definitions of "fun" is "violent or excited activity or argument." The very word makes me want to sit in a dimly lit room with lots of pillows—*by myself.*

It helps to think of introverts as people with sensitive night vision. We enjoy the comfort of darker surroundings, and there we are free to focus on the ideas that emerge. Pull us into the bright light, and our pupils close tight; we shield our minds from the harmful rays. Words like "party" and "fun" may turn us off, but try "intimate" or "casual," and we might want to hear more.

Extroverts worry when we hang out in the dark, sometimes for good reason, but often because *they* fear the dark. Internal space is more threatening to extroverts, so they project their concerns onto us. The introvert, in the meantime, may be quite content. We are more trusting of the dark. We know that, if we allow our eyes to adjust, we can see. We know that the stars are brightest when the artificial light is extinguished. And we know that, like the stars, some truths only emerge after the lights go out. We revel in a more muted light.

Introversion allows us to see what is less visible in the light: the world of ideas. Ideas, by their nature, start inside. They are original to the extent that they come from *someplace else*— from the "just right" mix of thoughts, and sometimes from dreams or sources we can't identify. Jung compared dreams to stars, warning that both are

> Q: What do you like best about being you?
> A: Resilience. I get depressed, disgusted, despairing, distraught, distended, disturbed, and deeply bummed. Two days later, I am playing guitar, mountain biking in the back-woods, meditating in the deep night, writing the story of my life, nuzzled with my daughter watching "The Big Bang Theory," and all is fine and good.
>
> —Doug, who knows his way in the dark

best seen *obliquely;* looking too directly causes the light to diffuse. The brightness of a star is dependent on the darkness of the sky.

Similarly, a dark mood can illuminate neglected realities, reveal what is not working, and inspire change. I love the phrase "sweet melancholy," because it captures the paradoxical comfort that comes with pondering difficult realities. The verb "brood" comes from a Germanic root referring to the incubation that leads to hatching. Rescuing a brooding introvert may thwart the birth of an original idea!

Introverts are drawn to mystery, complex ideas, and inner realities. If extroverts seek stimulation, introverts seek to be absorbed, to be fascinated. And, as we succeed in this endeavor, *we* become fascinating!

> *Hail divinest Melancholy,*
> *Whose Saintly visage is too bright*
> *To hit the Sense of human sight.*
>
> —John Milton, from
> *Il Penseroso*

INTROVERTS ARE COOL

Yin is associated with the coolness of earth, whereas *yang* holds the warmth of the sun. Extroverts want to heat things up; we like to chill out. We use words like "cool" and "chill" to refer to people who are relaxed, comfortable with themselves, and don't require a lot from the outside.

Introversion holds the ability to step back, cool down, and get perspective. Heat may forge, but it takes cool to clarify. When people get too close to the action, they lose perspective and get lost. As a psychologist, I help people develop the capacity to keep a part of themselves out of the action, unaffected, cool. When this observing capacity is strong, it gives us the ability to not just live, but to *know* we are living. While one part of us plays out the drama, another part gets to sit in the dark of the movie theatre and watch. This is how we make meaning; this is how we learn.

Introverts may seem cold as we pull away from the drama, but we're also the ones overheated extroverts seek out for perspective.

And just as the darkness exposes unseen light, the removed perspective of the observer invites the warmth of meaning.

WIDE RECEIVERS

Yin is often described as a feminine function, because it is receptive and open. In this context, "feminine" does not refer only to females; in fact, the introvert-to-extrovert ratio is higher for men than for women. Clint Eastwood would probably not be confused with a female, but he has a strong *yin* function. He describes himself as quiet, receptive, and open to new learning. He describes himself as an introvert.

Yet, the receptive function is no better captured than in the metaphor of birthing. Introverts take in raw materials and create something new. A writer takes in observations and creates a story. A scientist takes in evidence and produces a theory. A therapist listens and develops insight. The ability to receive and hold is essential to the creative process. The more receptive we are, the more complexity we can manage and the more we are able to integrate. The holding capacity of introversion gives ideas time to simmer, to incubate. When we give birth to ideas and books and inventions, we channel something larger than ourselves. We participate in creation.

THE YIN CELEBRATION

We celebrate introversion when we gaze at the beauty of a full moon. We touch introversion when we feel cool earth under bare feet and when we rest in the shade of a tree. We behold introversion in open expanses of nature and in uncluttered interiors. We savor introversion by candlelight and starlight, in the pages of a book, and in the meeting of minds.

An introversion party is three people sprawled on couches and pillows, reading and occasionally talking. Or a couple cuddling by a fire at camp, savoring the music of crackling wood and crickets. Your introversion party might be a solitary walk where thoughts are exposed to air and become clear. You might find your party in meditation, when time expands and everything seems possible. Your party might come with popcorn as you passionately observe the big screen of the theatre, or with a steaming cup of Ethiopian blend as you watch people from your table at the coffeehouse, or with a cold beer as you watch the world go by from your porch.

Notice introversion. Celebrate the subtle. Passionately wait. Make a date with the moon. Go barefoot. Tackle the tough questions. Have a really good conversation. Savor a glass of good wine or the delicate flavors of French food. Let an idea sit. Trust the dark and the unknown. Allow babies to remind you what comes of receiving, waiting, and trusting. Celebrate your natural specialty. And, while you're at it, raise a glass, mug, or whatever you have on hand to introverts everywhere, content in the knowledge that *this* celebration can take place *right where you are.*

> I use my thoughts to gain insight, sometimes empirically, sometimes intuitively. I often do not share my insight—for many different reasons. But while I often dwell in my own cave, I am not withdrawn in social situations and will readily reveal my opinions, display my abilities... For me, the excitement and action are internal.
>
> —Sandy, sixty and excited about her new career in technology

Chapter 18:
Expressing
What's In There

If you are not afraid of the voices inside you, you will not fear the critics outside you.
—Natalie Goldberg

While others chat, introverts listen, observe, analyze, and collect impressions. We also entertain ideas from internal sources: memories, dreams, reflections. In our minds, we work out theories, plan ahead, sort out what happened, converse, compose, draft, and design.

Sometimes we feel weighted down by all that is inside. As ideas become fully formed and take on significance, we want and need to express them. Sometimes, we have no choice. I recall a time during my analysis when my psyche was churning out insights at an unprecedented rate. And feelings—ones I had been too scared to acknowledge—were now available to me. On an ordinary day during this extraordinary time, my husband made the mistake of saying something that set me off.

I started *screaming*—not at him, though I was compelled to block his voice, to block anything more from coming in. The scream sounded foreign, and carried a power that both alarmed and satisfied me. I moved away from my husband, bent down on my knees. I knew I was supposed to stop; I had *children* in the house. But I didn't. It felt too good. I released another wave of raw, aggressive sound.

I'll never forget my talk with my son that night. I apologized for scaring him, but I also told him what I had learned: I had let too much feeling build up inside me, and I needed to find a better way of letting things out—a way that didn't hurt me or the ones I loved.

That was my only primal scream—except for the planned, collective scream I had joined during finals week at college. Perhaps I enjoyed my spontaneous scream so much because I knew I would never risk such a display again. But I have screamed on paper. I have screamed in plays. I have expelled power I didn't know I had in me.

I remember a particular play rehearsal: my character, a bitter, angry woman, was confronting the man who had abandoned her, pregnant, many years ago. The director kept asking me for *more:* more anger, more venom, louder, scarier. I was thrilled! Here was a place where my "more" was safe.

As my scream had revealed, I needed to find a *big* vehicle— or vehicles—for expressing myself. Introverts don't use the little vehicles, like small talk and rapid-fire conversation. Besides, we *enjoy* keeping ideas inside for awhile. But when we're ready, when the elements come together and we have something to say, we're *really* ready. In fact, we may feel ill or depressed if we don't get it out.

WRITING IT OUT

If Goth is an archetype of the introvert subculture, the writer is the archetype of the introvert. On the blank page, the writer's inner world rules. She can write *anything,* and nobody will interrupt or argue the point (at least until submission time!). Even when an author is not writing, she is living in her head, developing ideas or characters. And writing demands an extremely high tolerance for being alone.

Writing also demands an extremely high tolerance for holding. I use the term "holding," as I did in the last chapter, in the sense that a pregnancy requires holding. When introverts are accused of *withholding*, the life-giving aspect of holding, or "growing an idea," gets overlooked. Holding is such a natural part of writing that even our literary mentors often take it for granted. Manuals on writing emphasize the discipline of "pen to paper," or "fingers to keyboard," but attend less to the writing that happens in your head. Author Carolyn See is an exception. She starts her book, *Making a Literary Life*, with the instruction to hold:

> *The wonderful thing about your inner life is that it's your inner life. Think about your writing when you're making toast or suffering through a meeting at work or spacing out watching baseball on TV. Something's in your head, or your chest, that wants to get out. But keep it there for awhile.*

Introverts don't really need this advice; I include it to remind you that you're already halfway there! "Prewriting" is essential to good writing. But so is writing, and See recommends you hold onto your writing as well:

> *Write your stuff, hide it, let it stack up. Reread it. Don't worry about it. Don't look for perfection. To switch metaphors, your first writing is as delicate as a seedling. Don't show it to some yahoo who wouldn't know an orchid from kudzu.*

Whether or not you identify yourself as a writer, putting thoughts, ideas, and feelings on paper is a great way to get the inside out. Because cathartic writing, or *journaling*, is for your eyes only, you get to release what's inside while maintaining privacy. Go ahead, scream on the paper or whisper your secrets. It's your paper. Whether you just need to vent or have a book inside you, here are some tips for getting started:

- *Write daily.* Even a small chunk of time, fifteen or twenty minutes each day, gets your mind oriented to what you're putting on the paper. Just as small, frequent meals aid metabolism of food, small, frequent writing sessions aid metabolism of ideas. I tell my clients that the time *between* sessions is as important as the time *in* session. Therapy is most effective when the client has the capacity to metabolize ideas raised in the sessions, to come in hungry next time, and obtain more food for thought. Writing works the same way. The best writing generates *more* to think about, and more to write.

- *Make it easy.* Have your materials ready. If you want a special "container" for your thoughts, take the time to browse the aisle of journals at your favorite bookstore. I think of a journal in the way Mr. Ollivander of the Harry Potter world regarded the right wand: it will pick *you.* On the other hand, some beautiful journals are left untouched because the writer is afraid to spoil it. A journal is not effective if it inhibits the writer. Sometimes a cheap notebook is a better option. Or, look in the dollar bins at a large craft or discount store. I have found some lovely journals this way, and I feel free to waste as many pages as I want.

- *Write crap.* As Ann Lamott puts it in *Bird by Bird,* write "shitty first drafts." If you are writing only for yourself, the function is just to *get it out:* forget punctuation and grammar. Practice *not* editing. Write down your shopping list if that's on your mind, or write about why you don't want to write. See if you can "talk" on paper. Listen to your thoughts and record what they say. If you are writing for literary purposes, practice shitty first drafts, and go back and edit your work as many times as necessary.

- *Tell the truth.* This is the writer's mantra. You'll feel tempted to filter and soften what's inside you. Catch yourself, and write the raw truth. As Natalie Goldberg says in her inspiring manual, *Wild Mind,* "Writing is the crack through which you can crawl into a bigger world, into your wild mind." Take on the challenge of finding words for the truth, rather than making truth fit your words.

- *Write your pain.* James W. Pennebaker and his associates at the University of Texas have conducted extensive research on the benefits of journaling. His findings: if you want relief, write about your most upsetting experiences, write *through* the pain, and connect painful events with your life story. Getting to the tough stuff was a key factor in helping people feel better and move on.
- *Respect your writing.* If it is time to write, don't wait until you have time. Make commitments to yourself, and ask others to hold you accountable. You can commit to a certain amount of time each day, or to a quota. For her creativity course, Julia Cameron assigns three full "morning pages" per day and, for those wanting a literary life, See insists on one thousand words a day. Find what fits you, and fit it in.
- *Record life.* Anne Lamott emphasizes the importance of taking notes rather than trusting memory. Her advice: *always* carry a pen and some index cards. Jot down enough to remind you of your ideas and observations, then pull out your cards at your daily writing session and expand.

BEYOND WORDS

Are you a doodler? Do you salivate at the sight of paints and brushes? Are you looking for an unrestricted form of expression? Art and music go beyond words to capture what is inside.

The artist may not even know the meaning of his creation until stepping back from it in the end. Sometimes meaning does not emerge, only expression. The vast range of artistic and musical styles reminds us that the inner life is rich and exciting, and that there is plenty to go around.

The tips for writing apply to all art forms: make room, get your stuff, commit, and have the courage to create

> *Artists wear black to keep the paint stains from showing so much. But honestly, I like to be in the background. Black helps me feel that way.*
>
> —Mark Wolfe on why artists wear black

crap. Get a jumbo-sized box of crayons and access your childlike freedom of expression. If you want to get serious, pick up a guide to materials and techniques, such as *The New Artist's Manual* by Simon Jennings. If you don't like to paint or draw, cut out images from magazines, arrange them on posterboard, and create a collage. If you are drawn to the refined, take up calligraphy or grow a bonsai. Through dance or yoga, your body can do the talking. Sing your own song or pound on the piano or drums. If talk bores you, there are plenty of other options for self-expression. Find your language and develop it.

> I like music you can't classify, that you can't put in a certain genre, although they do it anyway. I like heavy, insane, beautiful, melodic, screaming. It can't stay the same the whole way though, it has to take you to different plateaus. Extreme bliss to infinite sadness.
>
> —Ben, musician and composer

Julia Cameron's creativity manuals, *The Artist's Way* and *Vein of Gold*, are great resources for helping you discover and express your gifts. If you're intimidated by artistic expression, surrealist painter Salvador Dali offers these helpful reminders: "Those who do not want to imitate anything, produce nothing," and "Have no fear of perfection, you'll never reach it."

HAVING THE STAGE

Yes, many introverts love the stage. This reality is baffling to many extroverts: "You must be an *extrovert*—you like to perform!" Extroversion has very little to do with performing. In fact, the expression of internal contents without interruption is a very *introverted* desire. Doing improvisational work may require more extroversion, but acting requires a good dose of introversion. Good acting relies on developing a character: a flesh-and-blood person with a history, a style, and a story. An actor also needs to be able to access memories of feelings and reactions and, as acting coaches point out, the ability to *listen* is key.

Performing, whether through drama, comedy, music, or dance, is attractive to many introverts. Introverted thespians enjoy the freedom of expression that acting allows, but also appreciate the protection offered by character and script. This is why the actor who is flawless on the screen may be awkward and rather tongue-tied during a live interview. Let's hear from some of our natural performers:

> *I [am] far more comfortable getting up and speaking or even performing before a crowd of people than most of the extroverts I [know]... But put me within a large social group where everyone is randomly interacting, I many times feel it's simply not worth the effort to make myself heard.*
>
> —Suzanne

> *For me, I get to hide behind my guitar.*
>
> —David

> *I used to perform in high school plays/musicals and loved it. It was an opportunity to be someone totally different. I would say introverts enjoy performing because it allows them to express...feelings, emotions...they would not usually express in their "real" life. I think sometimes the assumption is made that the introvert does not have these feelings or passions, but they do...they are just slow or loathe to express them.*
>
> —Karen

> *The stage is a place where I can assume...a larger personality than what I show in mundane daily life...My wife often remarks how reticent and reserved I can be sometimes on social outings, but put me on a stage and I become this much more "out there" figure. The stage is a place of unlocking those parts of myself I don't give permission—or am not given permission—to express in daily life.*
>
> —Doug

Comedy is my everything. It pumps through my blood. I love making people laugh, making them feel good, which is why I like to perform.

—Jessica

Even if you have no interest in getting on stage, the ability to assume a role can be extremely useful in stressful situations. If you pretend to be a more expressive person, the *character* can say what you script, while the rest of you watches.

INTROVERSION DIVERSIONS

As an alternative to releasing what's inside, a compelling diversion can help you out of your own head for a while. For me, there is nothing like a dark movie theatre and a big screen to pull me into a different world. Getting lost in a book, walking in nature, listening to music, meditating in silence—whatever it is, find your introversion diversion and let it take you out, regularly. Let's take a closer look at some of our favorite alternative realities:

> I have a bookcase inside my closet in my room, and I love opening the closet door and sitting in front of my bookcase, to either read certain passages, reminisce with certain books or notebooks, or just rearrange them. I never realized how books can be almost erotic.
>
> —Cecilia

Books, books, books! We can't seem to get enough of them. A good book is like a friend waiting for you at home, providing comfort and familiarity alongside excitement and adventure. In contrast to "quick fix" diversions, a book lets the reader inside. You have time to get to know the character—her thoughts and secret yearnings—to live inside of a story, or to master a subject. Through a single book of nonfiction, you can obtain inside knowledge gleaned from a lifetime of experience. And through fiction, you can inhabit another life, another time, even another world. Reading is like travel, allowing you to exit your own life for a bit, and to come back with a renewed, even inspired, perspective.

And books themselves, even unopened, have an enchanted quality, especially for introverts. I think this is because, in a bookstore, library, or next to a bookcase, we are with our people: thinkers, dreamers, others like us who relish time and solitude.

If a good book is a friend, some become lifetime companions—or as one instructor put it, your "soul books." The story that calls you back, over and over again, is like your greater Self, ever abundant and generative, yet completely yours. Discovering your soul book, or your soul author, is like coming home. Sure, you are fed and strengthened by the story. But, mostly, you just like hanging out inside.

Melting into the movies. Art, literature, music, and film all offer a bigger version of our experience, allowing us to fold inside something safe and relax. The elements of the movie theatre contribute to this embrace. You sit in a cushioned seat, comforting food beside you, in the dark womb of the theatre, and the Big Screen becomes your world. Ideally, you would have the theatre all to yourself, and I have actually enjoyed this luxury during some of my midweek, midday screenings. But even when the space is shared, anonymity rules, and other viewers soon become swallowed in darkness.

Many introverts prefer their movies at home, especially if the cinemas within reach are overcrowded. While I love the movies brought in by our local film festival, I often pass

> *Books and movies both create the same response. I can become part of either. If something embarrassing happens in a book or movie, I will actually blush. I won't even tell you what impact the line "Scarecrow, I'll miss you most of all" still has on me. (I've watched* The Wizard of Oz *a couple of dozen times, and I always identify most with the Scarecrow.) I've read* The Lord of the Rings *over twenty times. I can become so absorbed that once I read the whole trilogy in a single weekend.*
>
> —Dave

because I know too many people at the showings. But when I can be anonymous and melt into the darkness, nothing rivals the real thing.

You sit back and see a place: a bar, perhaps, or a front lawn, or a war zone. The filmmaker creates a mood through lighting, color tones, and the angles of the camera. You just ride. Whatever is on the screen takes on significance: the green of the grass, the heroine's lipstick, the sound of footsteps. In the safety of the theatre, you can laugh out loud and cry tears you have held too long.

After the credits roll, as you leave the theatre, you hold on to your perspective as a viewer. You notice things: people exiting and dispersing in various combinations, the coolness or warmth of the air, the snap of a car door as it closes. Your mind's eye is also sensitized: you reflect on the movie and on your life. From the perspective of the viewer, your life seems more interesting than usual, more significant.

This cinematic perspective is what inspired me to develop my version of "movie therapy," or what I have sometimes called "movie meditation." Here's how it works:

> Schedule a movie a week, and clear at least twenty minutes for post-movie reflections. Pick a show time when the theatre is less crowded, and go solo. Bring a notebook or journal if you like, and have a comfortable place to go, *by yourself,* after the show. Having a coffeehouse or café close by is ideal, or you may prefer to walk outside.

Then try it. Leave your cell phone off after the movie and savor the afterglow. If you have a journal, you might want to write your reflections, or begin the screenplay of your life. Try writing the scene around you and describing yourself in third person.

The practice of movie therapy can help you appreciate and enjoy the artistic value of your own life. In life, we strive for control and guarantees. In a movie, we *like* not knowing. Practice viewing your own life cinematically. Step back and enjoy the not knowing. When things get harder or life takes a turn, see the challenge as plot thickener and remind yourself that the plot *will* resolve. Notice the artistic quality of your day, i.e., how you get dressed or put on makeup, what you see as you walk to your mailbox, the expressions on the face of a loved one. Add music for effect.

Eclectic expressions. Introverts find many and varied ways of expressing and stepping back from the action inside. Here's a very small sampling:

- Studying languages is one of the most prominent ways I express myself. The way English words sound does not always express my ideas and feelings accurately. For example, *hermosa* expresses the word *beautiful* far better for me, but *hermosa* is Spanish. I've been working to close language gaps almost every day.—Solveig
- One quirky thing I like to do is visit cemeteries…I think they are beautiful. Not sure too many folks enjoy them, but I do. Especially if it is foggy and cool.—Karen
- Golf, lately.—David
- Running alone. This gives me complete control over path and speed. It allows me to shake up my thoughts and emotions—literally through movement. Running lets me express what is inside of me by enabling it to flow through my entire body…*I tend to move from running to writing to talking if I really want to express and understand what is inside of me.*—Beth
- [Watching], whenever possible, a major league baseball game.—Don
- I'm passionate about figuring out what my problem is and becoming peaceful. I also like little art projects like snowflakes, cards, and boxes. I love cleaning. I LOVE NATURE!! HIKING, OCEAN, LAKES, RIVERS, FIELDS, EVERYTHING!! I love one-on-one conversations. —Jessica

- Creating things like good meals in the kitchen and good letters for fonts on the computer.—Annie, font designer
- Crossword puzzles…Playing with and walking our dog and helping get dogs adopted at Arlington's animal shelter.—Ingrid

Though our discussion has focused on the personal benefits of self-expression, there's more to this story. Introverts paradoxically pull away from culture and create culture. We provide perspective that is seasoned by time and experience, nourished by thought and imagination, and fueled by desire. And our hungry society is ready to hear from us.

Chapter 19:
Moshing on Your
Own Terms

You have to systematically create confusion, it sets creativity free. Everything that is contradictory creates life.

—Salvador Dali

Ben is an introvert: thoughtful, rooted, "chill," yet kind and gentle. He has a calming manner about him and, in his presence, people feel safer and more relaxed. He's a big guy, and typically wears black; he recently traded in his dreadlocks for a cropped, jet-black haircut. His appearance may seem intimidating to strangers, but it filters out the ignorant. He embodies a beautiful mix of Shadow Dweller and Accessible Introvert. He's smart and he works hard, landscaping or delivering pizzas between his shifts as a lab engineer and production instructor, playing industrial metal guitar, composing, and producing. His music contrasts with his calm demeanor, as do his favorite bands. And Ben has been known to mosh.

There is no such thing as a "pure" introvert. We all have times when we want to get into the mix, even if the mix happens in bed with a lover, or at the family table in the midst of a heated political debate. My extroverted friend recently told me that I am more extroverted one-on-one than she is: I like a good argument with my husband; she prefers intimate exchanges to flow without conflict. In general, introverts become more extroverted when the group is smaller and intimate, and/or when participants share a common interest. A Goth may be reclusive during school, but at a party among close friends, he rises from—or I should say *with*—the dead.

But because of the ongoing pressure introverts feel to convert to extroversion, we reflexively duck when the topic of *extroverting* comes up. How do we maintain integrity as introverts, and at the same time allow our natural extroverted tendencies to emerge?

The answer: *organically.* We mosh best when we *feel like* moshing. The *T'ai Chi* symbol illustrates that introversion (yin) flows into extroversion (yang) and extroversion flows into introversion. Each specialty houses the nucleus of the other. When the introvert is safe, she can extrovert. When the extrovert is safe, he can introvert.

But note that, before yin flows into yang, yin *expands*—just as a wave swells before it diminishes. Pressure to *reduce* introversion can reverse the sequence: we deny the preference for peace and quiet and become stressed pseudo-extroverts. Then, as we get stronger and more confident, we give up the sham and return home to *introversion;* we don't venture beyond to extroversion.

A more natural sequence starts by going with what comes naturally—what generates the most energy—and riding it out. If we can't do this early, we do it later, but we deserve a chance to ride the wave as far as it will take us. This is why most of this book is about expanding and accepting everything introverted.

When we allow the natural specialty of introversion to lead, we not only expand our power, we experience fulfillment and satisfaction. Once satisfied, once we master the art of introversion, we might want to see what else is out there.

MEETING YOUR OPPOSITE

According to Jung's theory, the flow to the other side usually occurs in midlife—hence, the *midlife crisis*. By midlife, we feel established enough to get bored. We start to wonder what we've missed along the way. That nucleus of extroversion wants to have a go. We long for more than a specialty; we want to be whole.

In midlife, we begin to discover the opposites within. So, the story goes, the responsible family man buys a red sports car, and the conservative career woman takes up belly dancing. While this kind of response seems cliché, there is usually more going on. I work with a man who has handled his finances impeccably all of his life. He didn't make the mistakes most of us do, like stacking up credit card debt or forgetting to save and invest. He has achieved that enviable position of knowing that he and his wife will be fine, financially, whatever happens.

But this man does have a problem. He deeply resents people who squander money, who put entitlement before earning, who spend first and pay later. I told him one day: "You both have half of it figured out. The spenders have no money but know how to enjoy it. You have money but don't know how to enjoy it." When he realized that he could *learn from,* rather than resent, his opposite, his attitude changed.

LEARNING FROM OUR EXTROVERTS

According to Jung, we are attracted to the people we need in order to grow. These people hold parts of ourselves we are not yet ready to integrate. This works well, because an introvert's "dirty work" is often an extrovert's pleasure, and vise versa. My husband negotiates with salespeople, and actually enjoys the challenge. He helps me get around in the external world; he is my protector and advocate. I help him negotiate the inner world, providing safety through emotional storms. When I went through analysis, we both gained insight. When he bought a red Miata, I discovered "Miata therapy."

> Whatever you love, you are.
>
> —Rumi

There is great wisdom in attraction. When you feel it, you want to be around the object of your attraction as much as possible. When both of you feel it, you touch heaven—you touch wholeness. You both feel lucky, like you've hit the lottery. And in a way, you have.

In the other person, you recognize a quality you long for, but you just can't embody, at least right now. You don't *know* you have it, of course, but you do. My client did not see the spender in him, but he'd been saving for that part of himself for years. It is good, in a way, that he did not recognize the spender in him for awhile. Instead, he fell in love with a woman from a family of spenders, and they held that part of him. By putting the inner spender aside, he was better able to accomplish his goals. Yet, it would be tragic for him to deprive himself of enjoying what he had so faithfully saved. When I alerted him to the fact that his money, still unspent after his death, would likely go to people who did not earn it, he agreed and became angry at the injustice of this outcome. He said to me, "Now *that's* a good argument for spending it myself." He knew that, even after he and his wife were accounted for, there was a lot left to enjoy—or pass on. With no children, he was pretty sure any leftovers would go to the lazy in-laws that he complained about.

I had a similar wake up call as I approached forty. As a child, I received a lot of attention for my looks, and it wasn't always the good kind. I began to associate being "cute" with being dismissed, not taken seriously, with being unintelligent. So I downplayed my looks, determined to prove that I was smart. I got good grades, went to college, then graduate school, and developed a reputation for my smarts. At the age of thirty-nine, I fell forward on ice so quickly that my face broke my fall. And I broke my face, about five bones, and I still have tiny plates and screws in my skull from the reconstruction.

I was lucky. My facial tissue was intact, and the plastic surgeon masterfully repaired the breaks. Like my client, I realized that I *did* care about what I had downplayed—my face, my exterior. I also realized that my appearance was fleeting and vulnerable: could I afford a little vanity, a little enjoyment of this gift? The answer was a bold "yes!"

So, in a completely uncharacteristic move, on my fortieth birthday, I decided to give modeling a try. In addition to my newfound appreciation of my exterior, I was becoming bored by depth, tired of analysis, and the prospect of attending to the surface sounded refreshing. I changed my diet, intensified my workouts, and started paying more attention to fashion. And I got some work, modeling for locally shot commercials and print ads. I'll never forget a photo shoot where my job was to wear pajamas, lie in a bed, and sleep in various positions. I couldn't believe I was being paid for this! My sisters were concerned that this feminist who often shunned makeup had lost it. But I was actually *finding* a piece of myself that I had pushed away.

Most everything you detest in others will come back and kick you in the butt—if you're *lucky.* It is good to define yourself, and it is good to know when it's time to break out of the definition and get bigger.

But it's much easier when love kicks us in the butt. Desire bridges the gap between what we are and what we can become. The extroverts you love carry the sort of extroversion you want. My client's wife was not a spendthrift; she was generous, and my client admired this quality. Don't worry, you won't become that extrovert, nor will he or she become you. You will take back the projections of some of these qualities, and you'll leave others for the extrovert to cover.

Here's an example: My extroverted husband loves to argue. I was terrified of arguing as a young person: I was the good child, the good student, blah, blah, blah. But I really wanted to feel safe enough to be "bad"—to talk back, argue, show my edges. I married a man with very sharp edges. He loves to argue, he's okay with making other people uncomfortable, and he trusts the adversarial process—a born lawyer. I wanted to have that trust: I envied friendships I saw in the movies who could fight openly and get to a new level of understanding.

I was extremely attracted to my husband's edges. I saw a part of me I couldn't pull off, yet, and I wanted him around to do it for me. None of this was conscious, of course. I just wanted him. He carried my projected edges for a long time. But I've been taking back the projection, bit by bit. I still have no interest in arguing with salespeople—though I have surprised myself on occasion—but I love a good fight with my husband.

> *Lord, grant that I may always desire more than I can accomplish.*
>
> —Michelangelo

ORGANIC EXPANSION

The model of organic growth provides some helpful tips on how to expand. We do best when we start where we're comfortable, when the soil of introversion is well tended and fertile. Rather than using unnatural means to speed our growth, we draw on the elements that come to us in season and over time. Let's look at some examples:

- Really indulge in introversion, and you're likely to crave a little extra—extroversion, that is. You'll experience that movement of yin into yang. Consider, for example, traveling by yourself, far away from familiar faces, others divinely indifferent to you. Chances are you'll eventually find yourself open to and even initiating exchanges with strangers. Because contact is optional, it flows out of you—it's natural, easy, and probably quite pleasurable.
- Do it for love, when you can. I've shared the example of sticking out a party for my friend. I used introverted survival techniques to refuel, and I learned I could

endure my worst version of a party and even learn some things. When your desire leads you to give in this way, the loss of ego can be freeing. As I watched the hours tick away, I started to enjoy the submission. And the night gave back: the after party turned out to be just my friend, her dance partner, and me in an intimate club. We had the chance to talk, sip Godiva martinis, and listen to a singer who was a convincing incarnation of Frank Sinatra. I was even inspired to dance. I witnessed extroversion expand and then flow into introversion.

- Ignore "should"; follow "want." The word "should" is a good indication that somebody else's standards are involved. "Want" is within *you,* and is the seed of change. To know what kind of extroversion you want to add to your repertoire, look to extroverts, real or fictional, that you admire or find attractive. If you want to know your future potential, desire is better than a crystal ball.

- As the Buddha put it, "believe nothing." Introversion does not fully describe you, nor does any category. The road to healthy psychology is to get an identity then lose it. Then get another identity and lose that one. Seek truth and live by it.

- Know when you're stuck. Boredom is a clue. Addiction is a clue. Low energy is a big clue. Real desire promotes flow and expands you. Fear, sometimes *masked as desire,* constricts. You may feel compelled to stay locked behind your computer even though you are miserable there and all life has been sucked out of the activity. This is not desire; this is avoidance, a response to *fear.*

- When you're afraid of change, give birth a chance. In our society, change *is* scary. The American Way is exemplified by an impossible metaphor: "pull yourself up by your bootstraps." This "just do it" mentality is unnatural. Holding, growing, and birthing your way to change—nature's way and the *introvert's* way—seems to be catching on, however. A six-stage model of change, identified by researchers Prochaska, Norcross, and

DiClemente, has begun to be used in a broad range of settings, from smoking cessation programs to sunscreen use campaigns. The research shows that successful change starts inside, where the first three stages take place: pre-contemplation, contemplation and preparation. So if you want to get "out there," you do better when you build up your desire internally first. It's easier *and* it works better. So, don't just do something, stand there awhile first!

EXTROVERTING FOR ENERGY

Although introverts typically go *in* for energy, there is another kind of energy that comes when "in" meets "out," when *yin* meets *yang*. The release of this energy, called *Qi* or *Chi* in the Taoist tradition, underpins Jung's theory of introversion-extroversion. According to Jung, integrating opposites within the personality not only brings a person closer to wholeness, but frees up life energy. The more a person is able to tolerate paradox in search of truth, the less energy will be spent defending a rigid position.

Imagine a world without extroversion. It would be nice and quiet. We'd all have a lot of room. Life would move more slowly so that each introvert had a chance to speak without interruption, and to think before talking or acting. We wouldn't have downtowns or elections or contact sports. No one would ask how you're doing, only what you're thinking. Sound like paradise? Maybe, until you imagine this state of affairs lasting for weeks and months and years and decades. Something essential would be missing.

We may find it easier to imagine a world without introverts, because sometimes *our* world feels that way. We compete, we talk a lot, we have parties. But our world is also infused with introvert energy. Without introversion, we would have no books and no readers, no philosophies, theologies, or dreams. There would be sun with no shadows, day without night. Something essential would be missing.

The something essential is *life energy*—that intangible spark emerging from paradox, the conflict that forces a higher-level solution, the chemistry that allows male and female to join and make a third, and the integrity that allows introvert and extrovert to coexist and make a better world.

THE PARADOX OF THE PIT

The mosh pit seems an apt metaphor of our extroverted, capitalistic society, with dancers body-to-body, slamming and pushing. But this chaotic scene can be viewed differently. Here is Ben's description:

> [It's] like a tribal dance. It's not about hurting each other, too much. If you push someone over, you help them back up. There is no winner, everyone flows together, kind of like a swarm of insects. It gets you back to your primitive nature.

At first glace, the mosh pit is capitalism on crack. People are pushing their way to the front, stomping down the competition if need be. Within the mob, a circular vortex forms, and moshers slam dance inside. Because of the risks associated with moshing, Tom Berger requires users of his online instruction book, *In the Pit,* to indicate that they have read the following warning: "The only way to ensure one's safety at a general admission event is NOT TO ATTEND THE EVENT!" Though people typically come out exhilarated but intact, injuries do occur, and even deaths have been reported. But for introverted devotees, the pit is not about violence: it is a place to let go, to relinquish ego, and to meld with the mob. Everyone is welcome. People compete, but also cooperate. James Cook, in his online essay "Zen and the Art of the Mosh Pit," captures the paradoxical nature of the pit:

> To look upon the mosh pit for the first time is an affront to the senses...Without any regard for the music, a large

crowd shifts and swirls in front of a stage. Bodies move to and fro amidst random acts of self-sacrifice and enigmatic grace.

Cook's description of moshing captures the way competition flows into meditation. The pit mixes it all up: danger and altruism, aggression and unity. Everyone's dual energy is exposed: they knock down; they pick up. Jung would have liked the metaphor: opposites colliding at every level and generating energy. With the higher-level perspective of introversion, the chaos becomes a pattern, a shared energy.

As with the pit, smashing into your opposite is risky. But is it indeed easier to stay on your side, comfortably separate, or is it more natural to be curious, to investigate what is unknown—to move toward your opposite?

Jung would say "yes."

Chapter 20:
Introvert Power

It is in your power to withdraw into yourself whenever you desire. Perfect tranquility within consists in the good ordering of the mind,—the realm of your own.

—Marcus Aurelius

We live in a society that thrives on interaction. We grow up learning the games. We are told that we live in a place where, like the mosh pit, you play or lose. Sure you can sit it out and watch from the sidelines, but the action is in the pit. Playing is how you have fun.

This is what we are told.

But we also live in a society that thrives on ideas. We learn, not just how to play with others, but how to use our minds, understand our emotions, and generate our own solutions. We are told that books hold indescribable pleasure. We are enticed to explore new worlds, to embark on the solitary journey. We learn to figure it out, to think for ourselves.

This is also what we are told.

When I began this book, I wanted to resolve the paradox of meditating in the mosh pit—to emancipate introverts from the constraints of an extroverted society. But the reality of the mosh pit woke me up to something new.

An introvert does not merely slide into extroverted society and meditate there. She'll get pushed to the side, or trampled. Her meditation will not be recognized. Be silent in a group of extroverts, and they'll happily consume the space. Our power does not easily translate into contexts dominated by extroversion.

Introverts who enter the mosh pit may be moved there from within: a personal ideology is captured by and expressed through the music. These introverts become intimately connected with the experience of moshing before entering the pit. Many will be content to observe. Luke, another one of my moshing consultants, noted, "There are a lot of people who just want to stand there and listen, and get really annoyed at the moshers. They're the ones pushing them [the moshers] back in to protect their girlfriends." And some introverts jump in.

Entering, however, means accepting the conditions of the pit. Just read Berger's guidebook and you'll appreciate the importance of knowing what you're doing. Moshers mosh: they slam and push and sweat. The pit must be mastered before it can be transcended. Though moshing may become a meditation, there is no moshing without aggression.

So, is the message here to adapt first? Do we have to buy in?

No. The answer to the mosh pit paradox, to the question of how to be fully introverted in an extroverted society, is this: *relinquish the belief that society is extroverted.*

Our society is made up of a healthy mix of introverts and extroverts. Even my family, I now know, reflects this mix. Both realities are always present—mosh pit and monastery, yang and yin. Introversion is coming of age. It is no longer enough to complain that extroversion won't let us be introverts. *Of course* extroversion won't let us be introverts; extroversion does not know *how.*

But introversion will, and introversion abounds.

It is time for us, as introverts, to take ownership of our society. We are here in great numbers, we are contributing and we are powerful. Sometimes it takes an extrovert to remind us of this reality. Though I long assumed I was invisible in my big, loud family, my extroverted sisters argue the contrary, telling me that *I* am the one that gets taken seriously, that my quiet wields a lot of power.

Introversion is very compelling in the outer world. Visit a portrait gallery, and notice the faces that draw you in. The *Mona Lisa* poses, even smiles a bit, but she doesn't give it all away. She sits regally and calmly. Her portrait captures the beauty of introversion. And she gets noticed. An estimated six million people a year come to see her, and she now has a wall all to herself. *That's* power.

Being openly introverted will always be a paradox, like Mona Lisa's smile. But it is actually *in* the paradox—in the challenge of outing introversion—that we discover our power. Hold paradox and you become larger, more powerful. Here is some food for paradox:

- We think of meditation as something we do in private, usually in a lotus position. But meditation is actually quite portable. In their book, *Meditation 24/7,* Camille Maurine and Lorin Roche instruct: "The key to meditation is that you set things up so that you are restful. When you rest in loving attentiveness, the vibrating silence that's underneath outer activity can emerge." Take your restful attitude into the world, and practice seeing the space between and the silence underneath.
- The next time you go to a mall or one of those obligatory parties, see if you can find the pattern, the rhythm, and make it a meditation. Allow yourself to look beyond the small talk to our shared condition and longings. Let your presence offer the peace you so value.
- Take your mind with you. Practice the simple exercise of noting what you think and feel: "Hmm, I like this." "There is something wrong here." "Okay, this sucks."

Turn up the volume on your inner wisdom. No need to act on it before you're ready, just notice.

- Allow others to see your introversion. Instead of looking in the mirror and putting on a perky smile, look in the mirror as you contemplate. Get an idea of what you look like and feel like *on the outside* as you listen for what is inside. Are you taking your inside outside, or are you wearing an extrovert costume? What does your "inner wardrobe" look like? What would it mean to take your comfort with you?

- Practice "confident pausing." When I studied speech, I learned to respect the pause. A deliberate pause holds the audience captive. Introverts think before speaking, and need time *within* conversations to develop their ideas and responses. In my family, I got used to others chiming in, so I learned to trail off and make room for interruptions—this was *not* confident pausing. A confident pause is a clear break, and communicates the expectation that others wait. Try it. Start with low-stress situations. Stretch out time. Use public space for thinking privately. Act as if you've got all day. Feel the power.

- Withdraw more openly. State your introvert needs in the affirmative rather than apologetically. Assume others understand and that they're weird if they don't.

- Absorb the power of collective introversion. Attend a meditation circle or prayer vigil. Look for people behind the scenes. Read, and make company with books. As William Gladstone put it, "Books are a delightful *society*. If you go into a room filled with books, even without taking them down from their shelves, they seem to speak to you, to welcome you" (emphasis mine). The poet Shelley also frequented introvert society: "I love tranquil solitude/ And such *society*/ As is quiet, wise, and good" (emphasis mine).

Society is ours to choose, ours to create. I think meditation is an apt metaphor for introvert power. As Doug Imbrogno, introvert and facilitator of a meditation circle, put it: "Meditation allows you to not get swept away by the flood of thoughts and emotions, to sit by the side of the river, to watch the raging torrent and not get swept down." Though he was talking about the inner torrent, a meditative attitude distances the outer torrent as well, allowing you to witness extroversion without getting "swept down" by it. And others may opt to come your way.

> *The personal life deeply lived always expands into truths beyond itself.*
> —Anais Nin

Tribute to an Introvert

Over the past two years, I had the privilege of knowing a girl who struggled to make room for herself. She, like many introverts, loved therapy. Unlike many teenagers, she was unrestrained in her honesty. And she was in trouble.

This girl, blonde and petite, playful and smart, hated school. And her hatred was not your ordinary "school sucks" attitude that comes with questioning authority. My client hated school because she could not *think* there. The classrooms were noisy, boys harassed her, and she was not doing well. Drugs helped some—the illegal kind. She begged me to help.

The standard psychological treatment for school refusal is to keep the child in school—to desensitize her to the anxiety of being in school and to help her develop coping strategies. But, even as her psychiatrist and I followed this protocol, I couldn't help but think that my client's desire for the home-school option was well founded. This was a girl who used her own time to volunteer at an animal shelter, to write, draw, and create a vision for her future. She had big academic plans, and she not only had her career track worked out, but also collected pictures of her future dream house.

Her parents and I exhausted every option to try to create better conditions for her within school, but quiet was just not an option. Alternative programs tended to breed delinquency, and she was already vulnerable enough. The family was too poor to afford a private option. To my client's credit, she persisted—maybe she had no choice. She said she would give up school entirely to get away from the chaos she was mandated to tolerate. And, yes, she had the ADD meds.

I challenged her to put together a proposal for home-schooling and indicated that an essential part of the plan would be abstinence from drugs. She excitedly got herself a planner, worked out a schedule, and she and I created a formal proposal to submit to the school. Her parents, exhausted from the struggle, fully supported the plan, as did her psychiatrist. The homeschool option was granted, and she thrived. Relinquishing the drugs was not much of an issue; she did not need a change in mental state to work in a more hospitable setting. I will never forget the day she hugged me and without an ounce of self-consciousness, said, "Thank you. I *love* you."

Before the end of a wonderfully generative year at home, a very *happy* year, my client was killed in a car accident. It was three days before her prom—her school invited her to participate—and she and her boyfriend were on their way to pick up his tux. It was a rainy day on a bad road, and she skidded. Later, when her father talked with me about her tragic death, he found comfort in a simple truth: "She was *happy* that day."

> The truth which made us free will in the end make us glad also."
>
> —Felix Adler

MEDITATING IN YOUR MOSH PIT

Introverts have remained introverts despite incredible pressures to adapt. Recall that we are more than 50 percent, while the buzz says we are rare. We have been diagnosed, worried about, reformed, overstimulated, and interrupted. But as we persist in being introverted, society also benefits. Introverts have more internal storage space, so we can bring more into consideration. As we stubbornly make room for ourselves, reflect and wait until we are ready, we come up with the kinds of ideas, creations, solutions, and solid truths that render others silent. We baffle extroverts with our mysterious power, the "Where did you come up with that?" kind of awe.

Isn't it refreshing to know that what comes perfectly natural for you is your greatest strength? Your power is in your nature. You may not think it's a big deal that you can spend hours immersed in something that interests you—*alone*—but the extrovert next door has no idea how you do it.

Our gifts are not only evident in our ideas and creations, but in the way we live. By pursing the "more" that we need—time, space, thought—we wedge open new possibilities for everyone. We preserve solitary places, and also scout ahead, rendering the inner life safer for others. The "less" that we need—less formality, fewer people, less external stimuli—also looks good, especially to the overextended. As Don so aptly put it, "I can (and do) entertain myself without resorting to bungee jumping or swimming the English Channel; work, play, hobbies, rest, and a few intimate relationships don't generally require a great deal from others."

Extroverts may pressure us to get in the mix, but they love the calm we bring when we don't comply.

While it's not a good idea to sit in the middle of a mosh pit, your power will be most evident when you bring it into the middle of your life—when you bring *you* into the middle. Perhaps you'll find yourself, as I have lately, spending more time in the living room while *others* retreat to their rooms. Maybe you'll more openly daydream and allow a Mona Lisa smile to get people wondering. You might walk a little more slowly, ponder more visibly, and show just a hint of how excited you are for your empty evening.

The people in your circle are rushing, talking, flailing about. You stand still and chill. You observe and wait. People pressure you, and you stay. You stand still and chill. You observe and wait. As you rest in your introversion, people get quiet with you. They sense your comfort with silence, and they forget why they were talking so much. As your energy spreads, a hush fills the room. Nobody feels a need to do or say anything.

Bibliography

Acker, Kerry. *The Goth Scene*. New York: The Rosen Publishing Group, Inc., 2000.

BBC News. "Denmark: 'Happiest Place on Earth,'" July 28, 2006. http://news.bbc.co.uk/2/hi/health/5224306.stm.

Barrows, Marjorie. *One Thousand Beautiful Things*. Chicago: Peoples Book Club, 1947.

Baudelaire, Charles. *The Painter of Modern Life*. Translated and edited by Jonathan Mayne. Phaidon: London, 1995.

Benjamin, Jessica. *The Bonds of Love: Psychoanalysis, Feminism, and the Problem of Domination*. New York: Pantheon Books, 1988.

Benson, Robert. *Home by Another Way: Notes From the Caribbean*. Colorado Springs, CO: WaterBrook Press, 2006.

Berger, Tom. *In The Pit: How to Survive Mosh Pits and Bodysurfing!* Thomas J. Berger, 2001. http://www.moshing.org/abouttomberger.asp.

Breathnach, Sarah Ban. *Simple Abundance: A Daybook of Comfort and Joy*. New York: Warner Books, 1995.

Cameron, Julia. *The Artist's Way: A Spiritual Path to Higher Creativity*. New York: J. P. Tarcher/Putnam, 1992.

Cameron, Julia. *The Vein of Gold: A Journey to Your Creative Heart*. New York: J. P. Tarcher/Putnam, 1996.

CDW Newsroom. "2007 CDW Telework Report." http://news room.cdw.com/features/feature-03–19–07–2007results.html.

Cleef, Alfred Van. *The Lost Island: Alone Among the Fruitful and Multiplying.* Translated by S. J. Leinbach. New York: Metropolitan Books, 2004.

Cohen, Patricia. "Child's Play Has Become Anything but Simple." *The New York Times,* August 14, 2007. http:// www.nytimes.com/2007/08/14/ books/14play.html?partner = rssnyt&emc=rss.

Connery, Donald S. *The Scandinavians.* New York: Simon & Schuster, 1966.

Constantine, Helen. *Paris Tales.* New York: Oxford University Press, 2004.

Cook, James. "Zen and the Art of the Mosh Pit." *Interzones* 1995. http://www.altx.com/interzones/gangsta/mosh.html.

De Mente, Boye. *Japan Unmasked: the Character and Culture of the Japanese.* Rutland, VT: Tuttle, 2006.

De Mente, Boye. *The Japanese Have a Word for It: the Complete Guide to Japanese Thought and Culture.* Lincolnwood, IL: Passport Books, 1997.

Dowrick, Stephanie. *Intimacy and Solitude.* New York: W. W. Norton & Co., 1991.

Ekman, Ivar. "Globalization Closes in on Swede's Treasured Vacation." *International Herald Tribune,* August 20, 2007. http://www.iht.com/ articles/2007/08/20/asia/ sweden.ph.

Emerson, Ralph Waldo. *The Essential Writings of Ralph Waldo Emerson.* Edited by Brooks Atkinson. New York: Modern Library, 2000.

Eysenck, Hans J. *The Biological Basis of Personality.* Springfield, IL: Charles C. Thomas, 1967.

Florida, Richard. *The Rise of the Creative Class.* New York: Basic Books, 2002.

Gates, Bill, Nathan Myhrvold, and Peter Rinearson. *The Road Ahead,* rev. ed. New York: Penguin Books, 1996.

Gauguin, Paul. *Noa Noa.* Danbury, CT: Archer Editions, 1976.

Gayford, Martin. *The Yellow House: Van Gogh, Gauguin, Nine Turbulent Weeks in Arles.* New York: Little, Brown and Co., 2006.

Geisslier, Jeff. "U.S. Stands Apart from Other Nations on Maternity Leave." *USA Today,* July 26, 2005. http:// www.usatoday.com/news/ health/2005–07–26-maternity-leave_x.htm.

Godin, Seth. *Purple Cow: Transform Your Business by Being Remarkable.* New York: Portfolio, 2003.

Goldberg, Natalie. *Wild Mind: Living the Writer's Life.* New York: Bantam Books, 1990.

Gravett, Paul. *Manga: Sixty Years of Japanese Comics.* New York: Collins Design, 2004.

Harris, Rachel. *20-Minute Retreats: Revive Your Spirits in Just Minutes a Day with Simple, Self-Led Exercises.* New York: H. Holt & Co., 2000.

Honoré, Carl. *In Praise of Slowness: How a Worldwide Movement is Challenging the Cult of Speed.* San Francisco: HarperSanFrancisco, 2004.

Jacoby, Sanford M. "Corporate Governance, Risk and Inequality in Japan and the United States." http://www.harrt.ucla.edu/publications/workingpapers/JacobyCorRis.pdf.

Jennings, Simon. *The New Artist's Manual: The Complete Guide to Painting and Drawing Materials and Techniques.* San Francisco: Chronicle Books, 2006.

Johnson, D. L., John S. Wiebe, Sherri M. Gold, Nancy C. Andreasen, Richard D. Hichwa, Leonard Watkins, and Laura L. Boles Ponto. "Cerebral Blood Flow and Personality: A Positron Emission Tomography Study." *American Journal of Psychiatry* 156 (February 1999): 252–257.

Jones, Del. "Not All Successful CEOs Are Extroverts." *USA Today,* June 7, 2006. http://www.usatoday.com/money/companies/management/2006-06-06-shy-ceo-usat_x.htm.

Jones, Maggie. "Shutting Themselves In." *The New York Times,* January 15, 2006. http://www.nytimes.com/2006/01/15/magazine/15japanese.html.

Jung, C. G. *Psychological Types.* Princeton, NJ: Princeton University Press, 1971.

Jung, C. G., and Aniela Jaffé. *Memories, Dreams, Reflections,* rev. ed. New York: Vintage Books, 1989.

Keirsey, David. *Please Understand Me II: Temperament, Character, Intelligence.* Del Mar, CA: Prometheus Nemesis, 1998.

Kelley, Rob. "Most Satisfied Employees Work Longer." *CNNMoney.com,* April 12, 2006. http://money.cnn.com/2006/04/10/pf/bestjobs_survey/index.htm.

Kelly, Marcia, and Jack Kelly. *Sanctuaries: A Guide to Lodgings in Monasteries, Abbeys, and Retreats of the United States.* New York: Bell Tower, 1993.

Khamsi, Roxanne. "Wealthy Nations Hold the Keys to Happiness." NewScientist.com News Service, July 28, 2006. http://www.newscientist.com/article/dn9642.html.

Lamott, Anne. *Bird by Bird: Some Instructions on Writing and Life.* New York: Pantheon Books, 1994.

Laney, Marti Olsen. *The Introvert Advantage: How to Thrive in an Extrovert World.* New York: Workman Publishing, 2002.

Laney, Marti Olsen. *The Introvert and Extrovert in Love: Making It Work When Opposites Attract.* Oakland, CA: New Harbinger, 2007.

Lao-Tzu. *Tao Te Ching: a New English Version.* Translated by Stephen Mitchell. New York: Harper Perennial Modern Classics, 2006.

Lightman, Alan P. *Einstein's Dreams.* New York: Vintage Contemporaries, 2004.

Lindbergh, Anne Morrow. *Gift From the Sea.* New York: Pantheon, 1955.

Lischetzke, Tanja, and Michael Eid. "Why Extroverts are Happier than Introverts: The Role of Mood Regulation," *Journal of Personality* 74, no. 4 (August 2006): 1127–61.

Livingood, Jeb. "Revenge of the Introverts." *Computer-Mediated Communication Magazine* 2, no. 4, April 1, 1995, http://www.ibiblio. org/cmc/mag/1995/apr/livingood.html.

Lucas, Richard E., and Ed Diener. "Understanding Extroverts' Enjoyment of Social Situations: The Importance of Pleasantness." *Journal of Personality and Social Psychology* 81, no. 2 (August 2001): 343–56.

Lucas, Richard E., Ed Diener, Eunkook M. Suh, Liang Shao, and Alexander Grob. "Cross-Cultural Evidence for the Fundamental Features of Extroversion." *Journal of Personality and Social Psychology* 79, no. 3 (2000): 452–468.

Mainiero, Lisa A., and Sherry E. Sullivan. *The Opt-Out Revolt: Why People Are Leaving Companies To Create Kaleidoscope Careers.* Mountain View, CA: Davies-Black Publishing, 2006.

Maurine, Camille, and Lorin Roche. *Meditation 24/7: Practices to Enlighten Every Moment of the Day.* Kansas City, MI: Andrews McMeel Publishing, 2004.

Memory Alpha. "Vulcan Mind Meld." http://memory-alpha.org/en/wiki/ Vulcan_mind_meld.

Milton, John. *Complete Poems and Major Prose.* Edited by Merritt Y. Hughes. Indianapolis: Bobbs-Merrill Educational Publishing, 1957.

Myers, Isabel Briggs, and Katherine Cook Briggs. *MBTI Manual: A Guide to the Development and Use of the Myers-Briggs Type Indicator.* Palo Alto, CA: Consulting Psychologists Press, 1962.

Myers, Isabel Briggs, and Peter B. Myers. *Gifts Differing: Understanding Personality Type.* Mountain View, CA: Davies-Black Publishing, 1995.

Myers, Isabel Briggs, Mary H. McCaulley, Naomi L. Quenk, and Allen L. Hammer. *MBTI Manual: A Guide to the Development and Use of the Myers-Briggs Type Indicator,* 3rd ed. Palo Alto, CA: CPP, Inc., 2003.

Mullary, William. "Committee on Government Reform—Telework Consortium Testimony." *Quench: Telework's Virtual Watercooler: A Telework Consortium Blog,* July 25, 2006. http://quench.wordpress.com/ committee-on-government-reform-telework-consortium-testimony/.

NationMaster. "Crime Statistics by Country." http://www.nationmaster. com/cat/Crime-crime.

NationMaster. "World Values Survey 2005" (http://www. worldvalues survey. org/). http://www.nationmaster.com/ graph/lif_hap_net-life style-happiness-net.

Nordic News Network, http://www.nnn.se/.

Nordstrom, Byron J. *Scandinavia Since 1500.* Minneapolis: University of Minnesota Press, 2000.

Oldstone-Moore, Jennifer. *Confucianism: Origins, Beliefs, Practices, Holy Texts, Sacred Places.* New York: Oxford, 2002.

Pennebaker, James W. *Opening Up: The Healing Power of Expressing Emotions.* New York: Guildford Press, 1997.

Pennebaker, James W. *Writing to Heal: A Guided Journal for Recovering From Trauma & Emotional Upheaval.* Oakland, CA: New Harbinger, 2004.

Pine, Fred. *Developmental Theory and Clinical Process.* New Haven: Yale University Press, 1985.

Pink, Daniel H. *Free Agent Nation: The Future of Working for Yourself.* New York: Warner Books, Inc., 2001.

Planet Earth. DVD. Directed by Alistair Fothergill. BBC Video, 2007.

Prochaska, James O., John C. Norcross, and Carlo C. DiClemente. *Changing for Good: the Revolutionary Program That Explains the Six Stages of Change and Teaches You How to Free Yourself From Bad Habits.* New York: W. Morrow, 1994.

Quenk, Naomi L., Allen L. Hammer and Mark S. Majors. *MBTI Step II Manual.* Palo Alto, CA: CPP, Inc., 2001.

Ray, Rebecca, and John Schmitt. "No-Vacation Nation." Center for Economic and Policy Research (May 2007), http://www.cepr.net/documents/publications/working_time_2007_05.pdf.

Rechtschaffen, Stephan. *Time Shifting: Creating More Time to Enjoy Your Life.* New York: Doubleday, 1996.

Reid, T. R. *Confucius Lives Next Door: What Living in the East Teaches Us About Living in the West.* New York: Random House, 1999.

Reuters [Tokyo]. "Japan Proposes to Cut Suicide Rate by 20 Pct." *Reuters AlertNet,* April 27, 2007. http://www.alertnet.org/thenews/newsdesk/T187539.ht.

Rheingold, Howard. *Smart Mobs: The Next Social Revolution.* Cambridge, MA: Perseus Books Group, 2002.

Rilke, Rainer Maria. *Rilke's Book of Hours: Love Poems to God,* Translated by Anita Barrows and Joanna Macy. New York: Riverhead Trade, 2005.

Rufus, Anneli S. *Party of One: The Loner's Manifesto.* New York: Marlowe & Company, 2003.

Schlosser, Julie. "Cubicles: The Great Mistake." *Fortune,* March 22, 2006. http://money.cnn.com/2006/03/09/magazines/fortune/cubicle_howiwork_fortune/index.htm.

See, Carolyn. *Making a Literary Life: Advice for Writers and Other Dreamers.* New York: Random House, 2002.

Shulman, M. "Are We Facing a Generation of 'Internet Introverts'?" *AAP News* 12, no. 12 (December 1996): p. 32.

Sjöberg, Lore. "Grok Spock on the Auction Block." *Wired,* October 11, 2006 http://www.wired.com/gadgets/miscellaneous/commentary/alttext/2006/10/71930.

Steindl-Rast, Brother David. "Learning to Die." *Parabola* 2, no. 1 (Winter 1977): 22–31.

Storr, Anthony, comp. *The Essential Jung.* New York: MJF Books, 1983.

Thompson, Richard F., and Arthur H. Perlini. "Feedback and Self-Efficacy, Arousal, and Performance of Introverts and Extroverts." *Psychological Reports* 82, no. 3, pt. 1 (June 1998): 707–16.

Thoreau, Henry David. *Walden.* Charleston, SC: BiblioBazaar, 2007.

Voltaire. *What Is Goth?* Boston: Red Wheel/Weiser, LLC, 2004.

Walther, Ingo F. *Vincent Van Gogh: The Complete Paintings.* New York: Barnes & Noble Books, 2001.

Wahlgren, Eric. "Spreading the Yankee Way of Pay." *BusinessWeek,* April 18, 2001. http://www.businessweek. com/careers/content/apr2001/ca200 10419_812.htm.

White, Adrian. "A Global Projection of Subjective Well-being: A Challenge to Positive Psychology?" School of Psychology, University of Leicester, 2007, http://www.le. ac.uk/users/aw57/world/sample.html.

White, Edmund. *The Flâneur: A Stroll Through the Paradoxes of Paris.* New York: Bloomsbury, 2001.

Whitman, Walt. *Leaves of Grass.* Edited by Karen Karbiener. Washington, DC: Barnes & Noble Classics, 2004.

World Health Organization. "Suicide Rates per 100,000 by Country, Year and Sex (Table): Most Recent Year Available; as of 2007," http:// www.who.int/mental_health/prevent ion/suicide_rates/en/index.html.

Wuthnow, Robert. *American Mythos: Why Our Best Efforts to Be a Better Nation Fall Short.* Princeton: Princeton University Press, 2006.

Zielenziger, Michael. *Shutting Out the Sun: How Japan Created Its Own Lost Generation.* New York: Nan A. Talese, 2006.

Acknowledgments

I am so grateful for the opportunity to write this book, and for all the people who have sponsored this very introverted effort. Thanks to introverts Beth and Maschelle, who made me swear to write the book; to my awesome agent Jacky Sach, who ran with it. Thanks to my editor at Sourcebooks, Shana Drehs, who has loved this project with me and made my vision real.

I couldn't have indulged so fully without the support of my heroic family: Barron, my trusted first witness and editor, who held everything together, even me; Bjorn, who kept me sharp by challenging my thinking; and Josh, who insisted on being with me, quietly, as I wrote the last sentence.

Beth Wheatley, thank you for being the friend I imagined—Van Gogh should have been so lucky. And to Cindy Boggs, the extrovert I would party for, thanks for your unfettered loyalty and support.

A special thanks to the introverts who contributed their voices and enriched this book: core contributors Solveig Meyer, Cecilia Pérez Homar, Don Rollins, Ingrid Carlson, Philip Allmon, Julie Aadland, Douglas Imbrogno, Margit Carlson, Ben Schoper, Karen Carlson, Dave Miller, Beth

Wheatley, Jessica Schoper, and Suzanne Manning; thanks also to contributors Lisa Joseph, Sandy B, Luke Schoper, Donna Mahl, David Parker, James Meyer, Cathy Helgoe, Bruce K. Haley, Linda Arnold, Annie Olsen, J.C., Amy Williams, and Beth Helgoe.

I am grateful for the contributions of the stellar professionals at Sourcebooks: Peter Lynch; Dojna Shearer; Sabrina Baskey-East; Sarah Van Male and Cyanotype Book Architects; the Sourcebooks production team; my publicist, Paul Samuelson; and the winning teams in sales, marketing, manufacturing, and publicity.

Thanks to Allen Hammer and CPP, Inc. for helping me sort through the vast MBTI® research. My appreciation to Mark Wolfe of Mark Wolfe Design for translating inner life into art and for showing me my introverted face, to artist JJ Deakins for the voodoo you do to my website, and to Dr. Tim Spears, for helping me network between dental visits. Thanks to The Writers' Village for all your help—Jim Wallace deserves an editing medal of honor—and for being my people. Gratitude to my spiritual guide, Sister Molly, and to Julie and Rebecca, my real-life soul sisters.

Finally, to the family I sometimes needed to hide from: Thank you for enriching my life with your vibrant personalities, creative gifts and loving support.

Index

About the Author

Steve Payne Photography

Laurie Helgoe, PhD, is a writer, psychologist, part-time actor, and model—and introvert. She lives in Charleston, West Virginia, with her husband, two boys, and golden retriever. This is her fifth book. *Introvert Power* news and updates are available at www.introvertpower.com. The author's website is www.wakingdesire.com.